This is a faithful saying and worthy of all acceptation, that Christ Jesus came into the world to save sinners. – 1 Timothy 1:15

THE
FAITHFUL SAYING

Register This New Book

Benefits of Registering*

- ✓ FREE **replacements** of lost or damaged books
- ✓ FREE **audiobook** – *Pilgrim's Progress*, audiobook edition
- ✓ FREE information about new titles and other **freebies**

www.anekopress.com/new-book-registration

*See our website for requirements and limitations.

THE
FAITHFUL SAYING

15 TIMELESS SERMONS FROM MOODY'S NEW YORK REVIVAL MEETINGS

D. L. Moody

The Faithful Saying
© 2025 by Aneko Press
All rights reserved. First edition 1877.
Revisions copyright 2025.

Please do not reproduce, store in a retrieval system, or transmit in any form or by any means – electronic, mechanical, photocopying, recording, or otherwise, without written permission from the publisher. Please contact us via www.AnekoPress.com for reprint and translation permissions.

Unless otherwise indicated, scripture quotations are taken from the New American Standard Bible® (NASB), copyright © 1960, 1962, 1963, 1968, 1971, 1972, 1973, 1975, 1977, 1995, 2020 by The Lockman Foundation. Used by permission. www.Lockman.org.
Scripture quotations marked "KJV" are from The Authorized (King James) Version. Rights in the Authorized Version in the United Kingdom are vested in the Crown. Reproduced by permission of the Crown's patentee, Cambridge University Press.

Cover Designer: J. Martin

Aneko Press
www.anekopress.com
inquiries@anekopress.com
Aneko Press, Life Sentence Publishing, and our logos are trademarks of
Life Sentence Publishing, Inc.
203 E. Birch Street
P.O. Box 652
Abbotsford, WI 54405

RELIGION / Christian Living / Spiritual Growth
Paperback ISBN: 978-1-62245-740-3
eBook ISBN: 978-1-62245-741-0

10 9 8 7 6 5 4 3 2 1
Available where books are sold

CONTENTS

Preface ix

1. Weak Things Confounding Things Which Are Mighty 1
2. Faith 11
3. Courage and Enthusiasm 23
4. To Every Man His Work 35
5. Love and Sympathy 47
6. The Gospel 57
7. The Gospel to the Poor 69
8. Ye Must Be Born Again 81
9. The Son of Man Lifted Up 93
10. The Love of Christ 105
11. Grace 115
12. The Grace That Brings Salvation 125
13. Faith in Christ 135
14. The Compassion of Christ 145

Dwight L. Moody – A Brief Biography 155

PREFACE

This volume consists of addresses delivered by Mr. Moody at the New York meetings. These addresses will be found to exhibit the same force and freshness as those eagerly listened to by many thousands in this country.

As a suitable title for the volume, it was thought fitting to take two words from a striking text that well summarizes Mr. Moody's evangelistic preaching: *This is a faithful saying and worthy of all acceptation, that Christ Jesus came into the world to save sinners* (1 Timothy 1:15, KJV).

In a few weeks, another volume of Mr. Moody's addresses will be published under the title of THE UNSPEAKABLE GIFT.

THE PUBLISHERS.
LONDON, June 1877.

CHAPTER 1

WEAK THINGS CONFOUNDING THINGS WHICH ARE MIGHTY

God has chosen the foolish things of the world to shame the wise, and God has chosen the weak things of the world to shame the things which are strong, and the base things of the world and the despised God has chosen, the things that are not, so that He may nullify the things that are, so that no man may boast before God.
– 1 Corinthians 1:27-29

I want to call your attention to the 27th verse. There is just one sentence there I would like you to focus on: *God has chosen the foolish things of the world to shame the wise.* Then, in the 29th verse, He tells us why He has chosen the weak things: *that no man may boast before God.*

Now, if we are to have blessing upon the Word in this city (this was the opening address in New York), we must give God all the glory. I dread coming to a new place; it takes almost a week or a fortnight to settle down to solid work. The people are thinking of the choir, saying, "What a large choir!" and, "So many ministers!" "Surely, there is going to be a great work now, with such a large choir and congregation, and there are so many ministers." It is "not by might, nor by power," but by God's Spirit. We have to get our eyes off all those things. There will be no work and no blessing until this is done.

Now, we have not come with any new Gospel; it is the old Gospel, the old story. We want the old power, the power of the Holy Spirit. If it is anything less than that, everything will come to nought and be like a morning cloud – it will soon pass away.

I can tell you, before the meetings go on any further, who will be disappointed and who, years later, will say that the meetings were a failure: every man and every woman who do not get spiritually awakened themselves. If there is a minister here in New York who does not get spiritually awakened himself, he will claim that the work has failed. But I have never known a man who has been spiritually awakened say the work has failed. Nowhere that we have been has it been the case.

What we want to happen is to get ourselves down. If there is to be a true revival, there must first be a casting down of ourselves before there is a lifting up. It was only when Abraham was on his face in the dust before God that He would talk to him. It is then that God lifts us up and the blessing comes. There is no true revival until God's people are lifted up; until they are spiritually awakened. It will be superficial until then. It will be a counterfeit. If you attempt to begin working among the ungodly and unconverted before you are spiritually awakened yourself, God will not bless you. As the Psalmist says, when the Lord has restored to us the joy of His salvation, then we will be able to teach transgressors the way (Psalm 51:12,13). But God cannot do a mighty work when we are lukewarm or cold, conformed to the world, and do not have the Holy Spirit resting upon us. Here and there, we will hear of one converted, but the work will not be deep and thorough unless the Church of God is spiritually awakened.

Nothing that I have seen in America has rejoiced my heart so much as the work in Princeton. I think they have a *real revival* there. The president of the college told me he had seen nothing like it, and one of the professors remarked that he did not think there had ever been anything like it in the history of Princeton. I inquired about the particulars and found that they had asked for different ministers to come there and had been disappointed. Then the Christians gathered together and prayed for God to bless them. Afterward, one of the faculty asked them to pray for *him*. Right there, then, the work broke out, and there have been about fifty who were spiritually awakened and brought back who had wandered from Christ, and it looks now as if all of Princeton was going to be blessed.

Oh, that it may commence here tonight in our hearts – that we may be spiritually awakened first; and then how quickly the Lord will bless us! If you want to introduce two men to each other, you need to be near to them. If you want to introduce sinners to God, you must be near to God and to the sinner too. If a man is near God, he will feel love for the sinner, and his heart will be going out after such. But until we are brought near to God ourselves, we cannot introduce men to God. Somebody has said, "God uses the vessel that is nearest at hand." If we are near to God, He will use us; and if we are not, of course, He cannot.

Now, what we want is to be in a position which will give God all the glory. There are some things that at times make me tremble for fear the work will all come to nothing because there is so much manworship. We have to get rid of this manworship before there can be a deep work. We must sink self. If we can only get "I" down in the dust, get outside of our dignity, get self out of the way, and say, "Here, Lord, use me if You can; and, if not, use somebody else," or in the spirit of the wilderness preacher who said, He must increase, but I must decrease (John 3:30).

then the Lord will take us up and use us. Oh, let me beg of you to do anything you can to keep down this manworship. Let us look at the Cross, with Christ full in view, and then we will have men coming into the kingdom of God.

Now, we will go back to the text. It is the "weak things" that God wants to use. We want the great things, the mighty things, but God takes the foolish, the despised, the things that are not. What for? That no man may boast before God (1 Corinthians 1:29). Now, what is this written for, if not to teach us that God should have the glory, and that we are not to take any of the glory for ourselves? *That no man may boast before God!*

The moment we are ready to take our places in the dust, give God His place, and let Him have all the glory, then the Spirit of God will work with us and for us. If we are lifted up, and say that we have such great meetings and such crowds coming, and begin thinking about the crowds and the people, we take our minds off God. If we are not constantly in communion with Him, lifting up our hearts in prayer, this work will be a stupendous failure. You will find in all ages that God has been trying to teach His children this lesson – that He uses the weak instead of the strong.

That which is highly esteemed among men is detestable in the sight of God (Luke 16:15). When God was about to flood the earth, He wanted an ark built. What did He do – did He call an army? No, He just called one man to build the ark. In the sight of the world, it was a very trifling thing. Yet, when the flood came, it was worth more than all the world. The weak things of the world that excite our scorn and contempt, are the very things that God uses.

When God delivered Egypt, He did not send an army. We would have sent an army or an orator. We would have sent some man who would have gone before the king and laid the matter out before him in grand style; but God did not do that.

He sent this man Moses, who had been back there in the desert for forty years, a man slow of speech – and God said to Moses, "Moses, I want you to go down into Egypt and bring my people out of bondage." That is not our way. When the king looked at Moses, he ordered him out of his presence: "Who is God, that I should obey Him?" He found out who He was. God used the little fly and the little frog. The world looks upon the fly and the frog with scorn and contempt, but the Egyptians found them to be a terrible army when sent forth to do God's bidding.

We may be very weak in ourselves, but see what a mighty God we have. God likes to take the weak things to confound the mighty. He causes the worm Jacob to thresh the mountains (Isaiah 41:14-15). The fact is, we have too much of our own strength. We are not weak enough. It is not *our* strength that we want. One drop of God's strength is worth more than all the world.

There was that giant who, we are told, for forty days came out every morning and every evening. Down into that valley came the giant of Gath, every morning and evening, and he terrified all the army of Saul. The whole army was trembling; it was afraid. When David was weak in himself and strong in the Lord, they did not fear the giant. But you see, Saul and his army had taken their eyes off of God. When we get our eyes off of God, how mighty that giant looks!

A young boy came up from the country. He heard about this giant, and the young boy began to inquire, "What does this mean?" The Hebrew soldiers told him, and he wanted to go right out at once to meet the giant. The last man we would have chosen, but God's ways are not our ways. God will have the glory; that is the point. If it had been some great giant, then we would have given the giant all the glory. The young boy requires no armor of Saul; he just takes a few small, smooth, round stones out of the brook and puts them in his bag. He says to the giant:

You come to me with a sword, a spear, and a javelin, but I come to you in the name of the Lord of hosts (1 Samuel 17:45). Yes, he leaned upon the strength of God. Now just look at that! He is to place that little stone into that sling. God directs it, and the work is done. The giant of Gath falls. David was the last one we would have chosen for the work, though he is chosen of God.

What we want is to learn the lesson that we are weak, and that we do not need any strength but God's strength. Look at Jonathan with his small army! He says, The Lord is not restrained to save by many or by few (1 Samuel 14:6). It is not these great meetings that are going to do the work. It is not by might nor by power, but by the Spirit of God. But let me just impress this upon you – that it is weakness that God wants.

There was weeping once in heaven. John wept when the sealed book was brought out and there was no one who could open the book. He might have looked upon Abel, but Abel was not worthy to open the book. He might have looked upon Enoch, but Enoch was not worthy to open the book. He might have looked upon Abraham, and yet the father of the faithful was not worthy to open the book. There were Elijah and Daniel, and the holy men of the Old Testament, and not one of them was worthy to open the book. Some of the saints of the New Testament had entered upon their reward. There was Stephen, who was martyred; Stephen was not able to open the book. And it is written, John wept much when he looked and saw there was no one worthy to open the book. But soon a voice was heard, Stop weeping; behold, the Lion that is from the tribe of Judah, the Root of David, has overcome so as to open the book and its seven seals (Revelation 5:5). John began to look around to see the Lion, and lo, it was a Lamb. Instead of having strength, we want weakness. It is the Lion – the Lamb of Calvary. He overcame the Lion of Hell, He conquered him. What we want tonight is to ask God to give us of His strength, then how small these obstacles will look! When we are walking with God, how all these obstacles flee away. Go up in a balloon and look down upon some giant, and see how small he looks! Go up to the top of a mountain and look down on some giant, and see how small he looks! But get on a level, and how large he looks!

God takes the weak things to confound the mighty. When He wanted twelve men to introduce His gospel, whom did He take? Did He call the wise and mighty? No; He called a few ignorant Galilean fishermen. It was those men the power of God rushed in upon. They were weak in themselves, but strong in God. So tonight, if there are men weak in themselves but strong in God, what a work they can do! No other strength but the strength of God is worth having.

When God wanted Germany to be blessed, He gave power to one man. The Spirit came upon Martin Luther, and all Germany was blessed. When darkness and superstition were settling over Scotland, the Spirit of God came upon John Knox, and he moved all Scotland. You can go where you will in Scotland today, and everywhere in that country you will hear the name and feel the influence of John Knox. You can go where you will in England today, and you will feel the influence of Wesley and Whitefield, grand and mighty men. They did not rely upon their own strength, for the Spirit of the living God was upon them. They were mighty in God.

Look at that man Gideon. He marshalled his army of thirty thousand men to give battle to the Philistines. God said, "Gideon, your army is too great. My people would be lifted up, and they would take the glory to themselves." God said to Gideon, "You just say to the men who are fearful and afraid, 'Go home.'" And the Lord reduced the army twenty thousand, leaving only ten thousand men. But God said, "Gideon, you still have too many; if those ten thousand men get the victory, they will say, 'Look what we have done.' Take them down to the water, and we will try them again. Those that drink it up one way, and those that lap it up another, shall be separated." Then God took away all but three hundred. God said that was enough. "If I get the victory with those three hundred, I shall have the glory." I would rather have three hundred men in New York whose hearts are right with God than a host who take upon themselves the glory which belongs to the Lord.

I have no doubt but that some here will say, "There are so many obstacles in the way I do not believe you are going to succeed. You will not succeed in New York; New York is a very hard place." If God is with us, we will succeed. If we take God out of our plans, we will fail, and we ought to fail. Is not the God of our fathers strong enough to take this city and shake it as a little child? There is no skeptic in the city of New York but what the power of God can reach.

When we were in Philadelphia, we almost failed for a few weeks. The crowds were so great that many of those who attended the meetings spent most of their time in watching the people. For a long time we could not get their eyes towards the Cross. By and by, when the holidays came, the numbers began to fall off, and it was the best thing for us. This was what we wanted, so that men could think of God.

Now, my friends, do not think that anything is small that God handles. Look at that little cloud up there, no bigger than a man's hand; but that cloud was large enough to water all Palestine, and out of that cloud, the land that had thirsted for three years and six months obtained all the water that it wanted. Plenty large enough, if God is in it.

Let me say before we close, that what we want is—to get hold of God. Now, there are a great many people who lend their ears to other people. They never hear for themselves. They want you people to use their ears for them. Let us each go up for ourselves, and pray to God that we may get a blessing for ourselves. If the

Spirit of the Lord God comes upon us, it will take all eternity to tell the result. If the Spirit of God comes upon us afresh, I have no more doubt about the success of the meetings than I have that we exist. If we are cold and indifferent, then the work will be superficial. It will not be lasting, and will not be what many of you are praying for. Let us ask God that we may receive the blessing of the Holy Spirit. Let the prayer be, "O God, awaken me. O God, give me a fresh baptism. Impart to me the blessing of Your salvation."

God said to Elijah just before calling him up, "Go, anoint Elisha to be prophet in your room." If God calls us to a work, He can qualify us to do it. When the time drew near for Elijah to be taken up, he said to Elisha, "I will go down and see the sons of the prophets." It had been revealed to Elisha that his master was going to be taken away. They traveled together until they reached Bethel, where Elijah said, "You stay here, and I will go down to Jericho and see how the sons of the prophets are getting on down there." But Elisha kept close to him, and they walked together to Jericho. When they reached Jericho, Elijah said, "You just stay here, and I will go over to Jordan." They were on a tour inspecting the theological seminaries. Yet again, Elisha kept close to his master, and as they talked, Elijah asked, "What can I do for you, Elisha? What is your petition?"

"Well," said he in reply, "I want a double portion of your spirit." That was a very bold petition. He was asking great things. That is what God wants us to do – ask great things. They came to the waters of the Jordan, and Elijah took off his mantle and hit the stream: the waters parted, and they passed through safely with dry feet. While they were talking, there suddenly came a chariot from heaven to carry Elijah away to glory. And Elisha took up the mantle of Elijah and went back to Jordan. When the sons of the prophets saw the mantle of Elijah, they cried out, "The spirit of Elijah rests on Elisha."

May the mighty spirit of Elijah rest upon us tonight. Let us go to our closets, let us go to our homes, and let us cry to the God of Elijah – "Here I am, O God, use me" – that we may be ready for all His service. Oh that we may be weak in ourselves, that we may give all the honor and glory to Jesus; and if we do this, we will see how quickly He will use us.

CHAPTER 2

FAITH

Seeing their faith. – Luke 5:20

A little while before this, Christ had been driven out of Nazareth, where He was brought up, and had come down to Capernaum to live. He had begun His ministry, and some mighty miracles had already been done in Capernaum. Shortly before, one of the officers in King Herod's army had a son restored to health. Peter's wife's mother, who lay sick with a fever, had been healed, and Mark tells us that the whole city was moved; multitudes had come to the door of the house where Jesus was sitting, bringing their sick. In fact, there was a great revival in Capernaum. That is what it was, and it is all it was. The news was spreading far and near. Everybody coming out of Capernaum was carrying tidings of what this mighty Preacher was doing, and of His mighty miracles, and of the sayings that were constantly falling from His lips.

We read a few verses back that a man full of leprosy had come to Jesus and said: Lord, if You are willing, You can make me clean (Matthew 8:2). I want to call your attention to the difference between the man who had the palsy and the man who had the leprosy. The man with the palsy had friends who had faith. The man with the leprosy had no friends who believed he could be cleansed. We do not read of any leper having been cleansed for eight hundred years. Back in the days of Elisha (2 Kings 5), we read of a leper that was cleansed, but none since that time until now. Here is a leper who has faith and who goes straight to the Son of God Himself. And I want to say that if there is a poor sinner here tonight who has no friends who would pray for him, such a one can go directly to Jesus Himself. You do not need any bishop or priest or potentate to intercede. This poor leper came right to Christ. He said: *Lord, if You are willing, You can make me clean* (Matthew 8:2).

There is faith for you. He did not say, like the man in the 22nd verse of the 9th chapter of Mark: *If You can do anything, take pity on us*. He put the "if" in the wrong place. But this leper said, *If You are willing, You can*. This pleased the Lord, and He said: *I am willing; be cleansed* (Matthew 8:3). and away went the leprosy. The man was made well in a minute. Of course, this news had gone out of Capernaum; and not only the city was stirred, but the country also. And now we read that people were coming up from all parts of Judea, from Galilee, and all the villages, even from Jerusalem. The news had reached Jerusalem, and the Pharisees, philosophers, and wise men were coming up to this northern town to see what this great revival meant.

They did not come up to get a blessing. Like a great many who come to these meetings, they came out of curiosity. They came to see how it was that this Man was performing such mighty miracles, and they were told that He was in the house. They went in and sat around the Master, and we are told, the power of the Lord was present for Him to perform healing (Luke 5:17) But we are not told that they were healed. They did not think that they were sick and needed a Savior. They were like hundreds now, who are drawing around them their filthy rags of selfrighteousness, thinking they are good enough without salvation. They just come here to reason out the philosophy of the meetings, and how it is that so many people come together night after night to hear this old gospel, which has been preached for 1800 years.

And the power of the Lord was present for Him to perform healing. I have thought a number of times what a glorious thing it would have been if they had all been healed. What a glorious thing it would have been if those men from Judea had been converted and gone back to publish the glad tidings in their homes and villages! What a revival it would have been! But the Pharisees and doctors did not come *for* that purpose, but only to reason out the thing.

While these things were happening, suddenly there was a noise overhead. The people heard a noise on the roof and looked up to see what was the matter. Now, there were four men in Capernaum – I have an idea that they were young converts – who had found a man with the palsy, and they could not get him to Jesus. Matthew, Mark, and Luke all give an account, but none of them says that the man himself had any faith. I can imagine these men saying to the man with the palsy, "If we can get you to Jesus, all He has to do is to speak, and the palsy will be gone." And I fancy I can see these men making arrangements to take this man with the palsy to Christ. They prepared a couch, probably something like the stretchers we had in the war, and I can imagine each of them taking his place to carry that couch through the streets of Capernaum. They go with a firm step and a steady tread. They are moving toward that house where Christ is. These men have confidence. They know that the Son of God has power to heal this man, and they say, "If we can only get him to Jesus, the work will be done."

While the philosophers, scribes, and wise men were there,

trying to reason out the philosophy of the thing, these men arrived at the door and could not get in because of the crowd. They undoubtedly asked some of the men inside to come out and let this man with the palsy in, but they could not get any of the people out – so there they were. But faith looks over obstacles. Faith is not going to surrender. These men felt they *must get in* in some way.

I can imagine they went to one of the neighbors and said, "Just allow us to use your stairway; here is a man with the palsy and we want to get him in." I can picture them taking this man up, until they finally get him up on the roof of the house where Christ is preaching. Now, you can hear them ripping up the roof, and everybody looks up to see what the noise is. At last, they see that while Christ is preaching, these men are making a hole large enough to let the man down through.

The owner of that house must have been a good man, or he would have complained to see his roof torn up in that way. But these men wanted to get the palsied man healed. That was worth more than the roof. They wanted to get him blessed. They let the man down right into the presence of those Pharisees and scribes. It would have been like letting him down into an icehouse, if Christ had not been there. Those scribes and Pharisees – they had no compassion; they had no sympathy for the fallen; they had no sympathy for the erring. There was One who had sympathy for the man who was suffering. Right down at the feet of Jesus they laid the palsied man. My friends, you cannot take palsied souls to a better place than to the feet of Jesus.

They called upon the crowd to stand aside and make room, and they just placed him at the feet of Jesus. Christ looks up, and as it is written in the 20th verse of the 5th chapter of Luke, *Seeing their faith* – not the man's faith; we are not told that he had any – He saw *their* faith – that is the point. I believe that this whole miracle is to teach us one precious lesson: to show us Christians that God will honor our faith. I see the Son of God looking up at those men who let this sufferer down. He looked up yonder and saw their faith. There is nothing on this earth that pleases Him so much as faith. Wherever He finds faith, it pleases Him. Twice Christ marveled. I believe Christ marveled only twice. Once He marveled at the faith of the Centurion, and He marveled at the unbelief of the Jews (Matthew 8:10; Mark 6:6).

When He saw their faith, He said to the man gazing at Him, Take courage, son; your sins are forgiven (Matthew 9:2). The man did not come expecting this; he only sought to get rid of his palsy. He did not expect to have his sins forgiven. These men began to look around with amazement. "That is a very grievous thing; He forgives sin. What right has He to do that? It is God, and God alone, who does that." I tell you the Jews did not believe in the divinity of Jesus Christ. They began to reason among themselves, but Christ knew what they were thinking about. He could read their thoughts. Christ said to them, Which is easier, to say, "Your sins are forgiven," or to say, "Get up, and walk"? But so that you may know that the Son of Man has authority on earth to forgive sins – then He said to the paralytic, "Get up, pick up your bed and go home" (Matthew 5:5-7). Now the man was palsied: he did not have the power to rise. But he leaps up in a minute. He packs up that old bed that he had lain on for years, and away he goes. The man walks out with his bed on his back, and away he goes home. The men begin to look at each other with amazement, and one and another says, *We have seen remarkable things today* (Luke 5:26).

How long did it take the Lord Jesus Christ to heal that man? Some men say, "Oh, we don't believe in instantaneous conversions." How long did it take the Lord to heal the palsied man? One word, and away went the palsy. One word, and the man stood up, rolled up his bed up, and away he went on his way home. I would like to have seen his wife. I can imagine she was about as surprised as any woman you ever saw.

But now the word I want to call your attention to is this: *Seeing their faith*. Now, there are a great many men in New York that have no faith at all in the gospel. They do not believe in the Bible. There are a great many men in New York who are infidels. There are a great many skeptics. There is one thing that encourages me very much: The Lord can honor our faith and raise those men. *Seeing their faith*.

Suppose a man would go to the house of his neighbor and say, "Come, let us take neighbor Levi to neighbor Peter's house; Christ is there, and we can get him healed." They find they are not able to carry the man, so they get a third, and the three are still not able, so they get a fourth. Now, I do not know of anything that would arouse a man quicker than to have four people combine to try to bring him to Christ. Suppose one man calls upon him after breakfast; he does not think much about it, as someone has invited him to Christ before. Suppose before dinner, the second man comes and says, "I want to lead you to Christ; I want to introduce you to the Son of God." The man has become quite aroused by now; perhaps he has never before had the subject presented to him by two different men in one day. But the third man comes, and the man is thoroughly alive by this time, and he says to himself, "Why, I never thought so much about my soul as I have today." But before the man goes to bed at night, the fourth man has come, and I will guarantee that he will not sleep much that night – with four men trying to bring him to Christ. If we cannot bring our friends to Christ, let us get others to help us. If four men will not do it, let us add the fifth. The Lord will see our faith, and the Lord will honor our faith, and we will see our friends brought to the Son of God.

When I was at Nashville during our late war, I was closing the noon prayer meeting one day when a great, strong man came up to me, trembling from head to foot. He took a letter out of his pocket and wanted me to read it. It was a letter from his sister. In the letter, the sister stated that every night as the sun went down, she went down on her knees to pray for him. She was six hundred miles away. The soldier said, "I never thought of my soul until last night; I have stood before the cannon's mouth, and it never made me tremble; but, sir, I haven't slept a wink since I got that letter." I think there are many Christians here who understand what that letter meant. The Lord had seen her faith. It was God honoring faith, and it was God answering prayer. And so, my hearers, if God sees our faith, those friends we are anxious for will be brought to Christ.

When we were in Edinburgh, a man came to me and said, "Over yonder is one of our most prominent infidels in Edinburgh. I wish you would go over and speak to him." I took my seat beside him and asked if he was a Christian. He laughed at me and replied that he did not believe in the Bible. "Well," I said, after talking for some time, "will you let me pray with you? Will you let me pray for you?" "Yes," said he, "just pray and see *if* God will answer your prayer. Now let the question be decided." "Will you kneel?" "No, I won't kneel. Whom am I going to kneel before?" He said it with considerable sarcasm. I knelt down and prayed beside the infidel. He sat very straight, so that the people would understand that he was not at all in sympathy with my prayer. After I finished, I said, "Well, my friend, I believe that God will answer my prayer, and I want you to let me know when you are saved." "Yes, I will let you know when I am saved" – all with considerable sarcasm.

At last, up at Wick, at a meeting in the open air one night, on the outskirts of the crowd, I saw the Edinburgh infidel. He said, "Didn't I tell you God wouldn't answer your prayer?" I said, "The Lord will answer my prayer yet." I had a few minutes' conversation with him and left him. But just a year ago this month, when we were preaching in Liverpool, I received a letter from one of the leading pastors of Edinburgh, stating that the Edinburgh infidel had found his way to Christ. He wrote an interesting letter, saying how God had saved him. There may be many in the city of New York who will laugh at the idea, and they will quibble, and perhaps they will say tonight that God does not answer prayer; but He does, if Christians will only have faith. God can save the greatest infidel, the greatest skeptic, the greatest drunkard. What we want is to have faith. Oh, let that word sink down deep into the heart of every Christian here tonight, and let us show our faith by our works.

Let us go out and bring all our friends here; and if the preaching is poor, we can bring down from heaven the necessary blessing without good preaching. In Philadelphia, a skeptic came in just out of curiosity. He wanted to see the crowd, and he had not more than crossed the threshold of the door before the Spirit of God met him. I asked him if there was anything in the sermon that influenced him, in hopes that I was about to get something to encourage me; but he could not tell what the text was. I asked him if it was the singing, but he did not know what Mr. Sankey had sung. It was *the power of God* alone that converted him, and that is what we want in these meetings. If we have this power, when we invite our friends here, the Lord will meet them and will answer prayer and save them. Let us bring our unconverted friends here. All through the services, let us be lifting up our hearts in prayer: "God save our friend! O God, convert him!" And in answer to our prayer, the Lord will save.

While I was in London there was a man way off in India – a godly father – who had a son in London. The father obtained a furlough and came right from India to England to see after his boy's spiritual welfare. Do you think God let that man come thus far without honoring that faith? No. He converted that son. That is what we want – faith and works going together; and if we have faith, God will honor it and answer our prayer.

Only a few years ago, in the city of Philadelphia, there was a mother who had two sons. They were just going as fast as they could to ruin; they were breaking her heart. She went into a little prayer meeting and got up and presented them for prayer. They had been on a drunken spree or had just started in that way, and she dreaded that their end would be a drunkard's grave; so she went among these Christians and said, "Won't you just cry to God for my two boys?" The next morning, those two boys had made an appointment to meet each other at the corner of Market and Thirteenth streets – though they knew nothing about our prayer meeting. One of them, who had been waiting at the comer for his brother to come, followed the people who were flooding into the depot building, where the Spirit of the Lord met him, and he was wounded of heart and found his way to Christ. When the brother came, he found the place too crowded to enter, so he went out of curiosity into another meeting, where he found Christ, and went home happy. When the eldest son arrived at home, he told his mother what the Lord had done for him, and the second son soon came in with the same tidings. I heard one get up afterwards to tell his experience in the young converts' meeting, and no sooner had he told the story than the other arose and said: "I am that brother; and there is not a happier home in Philadelphia than ours," and they went out, bringing their friends to Christ.

Let us now show our faith by our works. Let us go to our friends, to our neighbors, and to those over whom we have any influence, and let us talk to them about Christ, and let us plead with God that they may be converted; and let our prayers go up to God in our homes and around our family altars. Then, instead of there being a few thousands converted in New York, tens of thousands will be converted. Let the prayer go up, "O God, save my unconverted husband." "O God, save my unconverted wife." "O God, save my unconverted children." And God will hear that cry.

As I was coming out of a daily prayer meeting in one of our Western cities, a mother came up to me and said, "I want you to see my husband and ask him to come to Christ." I took out my memorandum book, and I put down his name. She continued, "I want you to go and see him." I knew the name; it was that of a learned judge. I told her, "I cannot argue with your husband. He is a good deal older than I am, and it would be out of place. Then I am not much skilled in infidel argument." "Well, Mr. Moody," she said, "that is not what he wants. He has had enough of that. Just ask him to come to the Savior." She urged me so vehemently, that I consented to go.

I went up to the office where the judge was doing business and told him what I had come for. He laughed at me. "You are very foolish," he said, and began to argue with me. I replied, "I do not think it will be profitable for me to hold an argument with you. I have just one favor I want to ask, and that is that when you are converted, you will let me know." With a good deal of sarcasm, he replied, "Yes, I will do that. When I am converted, I will let you know." In that moment, I had faith that the prayers of his wife would be answered if mine were not.

A year and a half later, I was in that city when a servant came to my door and said, "There is a gentleman in the drawing room waiting to see you." I found the judge there. He said, "I promised I would let you know when I was converted." While I had heard of his conversion from other lips, I rejoiced to hear of it from his own. He shared that his wife had gone to a meeting one night, leaving him at home alone. While he was sitting there by the fire, he began to think, "Supposing my wife is right, and my children are right: suppose there is a heaven and hell, and I will be separated from them." His first thought was, "I don't believe a word of it." The second thought came, "You believe in the God that created you, and that the God who created you is able to teach you. You believe that God can give you life."

The judge continued, "Yes, the God that created me can give me life. I was too proud to get down on my knees by the fire, but I said, 'O God, teach me.' And as I prayed, I do not understand it, but it began to get very dark, and my heart felt very heavy. I was afraid to tell my wife, so when she returned I pretended to be asleep. She knelt down beside the bed, and I knew she was praying for me. I kept crying, 'O God, teach me.' I had to change my prayer to, 'O God, save me; O God, take away this burden.' But it grew darker and darker, and the load grew heavier and heavier. All the way to my office I kept crying, 'O God, take away this load.' I gave my clerks a holiday, and just closed my office and locked the door. I fell down on my face, and cried in agony to the Lord, 'O Lord, for Christ's sake, take away this guilt.' I do not know how it was, but it began to grow very light. I said, 'I wonder if this is what they call conversion. I think I will go and ask the minister if I am not converted.'" The old judge then said to me, "Mr. Moody, I have enjoyed life in the last three months more than all the previous time put together."

The judge did not believe, but his wife did, and God honored her faith and saved that man. He went up to Springfield, Illinois, where he stood before the politicians and talked about what God, for Christ's sake, had done for him.

Now let this text sink down deep into your hearts: *Seeing their faith.*

Let us lift up our hearts to God in prayer that He may give us faith.

CHAPTER 3

COURAGE AND ENTHUSIASM

Be strong and courageous. – Joshua 1:6, 7, 9, 18

I will take for my subject tonight only two words: *courage* and *enthusiasm* – necessary qualifications for successful work in the Lord's service. It is in this chapter (Joshua 1) that I read tonight, four different times does God tell Joshua to be of good courage; He says that if he was courageous, no man would be able to stand before him all the days of his life. And we read that Joshua was very successful, and that no man was able to stand before him all his days. God fulfilled His promise. God kept His word.

But see how careful God is to instruct him on this one point. Four times in one chapter He says to him, "Be courageous"; and then follows the promise that he shall prosper, and shall have good success. And I have yet to find that God ever uses a man who is all the time looking on the dark side, and talking about the obstacles, and looking at them, and who is discouraged and cast down. It is not those Christians who go about with their heads hanging down like bulrushes, looking at the obstacles and talking about the darkness all the time, whom

God uses. They kill everything they touch. There is no life in them. Now, if we are going to succeed, we have to be courageous. The moment we get our eyes on God and remember who He is, that He has all power in heaven and earth, and that it is God who commands us to work in His vineyard, then it is that we shall have courage given us.

Now, if you will take your Bibles and look carefully through them, you will see that the men who have left their mark behind them – that the men who have been successful in winning souls to Christ – have all been men of courage. You will notice that after Moses had been among the Egyptians for forty years, he thought the time had come for him to commence his work of delivering the captives. He went out, and the first thing we hear is that he was looking this way and that way to see if somebody saw him. He was not fit for God's work. God had to take him on the back side of the desert for forty years. Only then was God ready to send him, and by that time, Moses looked but one way. When God sent him down into Egypt, he had boldness; he went right before the King of Egypt. He had courage, and God could use him. But it took him forty years to learn that lesson – that he must have courage and boldness to be a fit vessel for the Master's use.

Again, we find Elijah on Mount Carmel, full of boldness. How the Lord used him! How the Lord stood by him! How the Lord blessed him! He was not afraid of Ahab and the whole royalty, and he was not afraid of the whole nation. He stood alone on Mount Carmel. See what courage he had, and how God honored him! But when he took his eyes off the way, and Jezebel sent a message to him that she would have his life, he was afraid. What came over him I cannot tell, unless it was that he turned his eyes away from the Lord, and when a woman sent him that threatening message, he became frightened. God had to speak to him and ask him what he was doing, for he was unfit for God's service.

That, I think, is the trouble with a good many of God's people. They get frightened and are afraid to speak to men about their souls. They lack moral courage. If they hear the voice of God saying to them, "Run and speak to that young man," they will go to him meaning to do so, but end up talking to him about everything else, never daring to speak to him about his soul.

When we begin to invite men to Christ, the work begins. It will not, however, begin until we have courage given us and are ready to go and speak with men about their souls. We read that when the apostles were brought before the Council, the members perceived their boldness, and it made an impression on them (Acts 4:13). The Lord could use them then, because they were fearless and bold. Look at Peter at Pentecost, when he charged the murder of the Son of God upon the Jews (Acts 2:36). A little while before, he had gotten out of communion, and one little maid had scared him nearly out of his life, so that he swore he did not know Christ. Ah! He had taken his eyes off the Master, and the moment we take our eyes off Christ, we become disheartened, and then God cannot use us.

I remember a few years ago feeling discouraged, as I could not see much fruit of my work. One morning, as I was in my study, cast down, one of my Sunday school teachers came in and wanted to know what I was discouraged about. I told him I could see no results from my work. He then asked, "By the way, did you ever study the character of Noah?" I felt that I knew all about that and told him that I was familiar with it, and he said, "Now, if you never studied Noah's history and character carefully, you ought to do it, for I cannot tell you what a blessing it has been to me." When he went out, I took down my Bible and commenced reading about Noah, and the thought came stealing over me: "Here is a man who toiled and worked for a hundred years and did not get discouraged; if he did, the Holy Spirit did not put it on record." The clouds lifted, and I arose and said, "If the Lord wants me to work without any fruit, I will work on."

I went down to the Noon prayer meeting, and when I saw the people coming to pray, I said to myself, "Noah worked a hundred years, and he never saw a prayer meeting outside of his own family." Very soon, a man stood up right across the aisle where I was sitting and said that he had come from a little town where a hundred people had united with the Church of God the year before. And I thought to myself, "What if Noah had heard that! He preached so many, many years and did not get a convert; yet he was not discouraged." Then a man got up right behind me, and he trembled as he said, "I am lost; I want you to pray for my soul." And I said, "What if Noah had heard that! He worked for a hundred and twenty years and never had a man come to him and say that; yet he did not get discouraged." And I made up my mind then that, God helping me, I would never be discouraged; I would do the best I could and leave the results with God. And it has been a wonderful help to me.

And so let me say to the Christians of New York that we must expect good results and never get discouraged; but if we do not get good results, let us not look on the dark side, but keep on praying, and in the fulness of time the blessing of God will come. What we want is to have the Christians come out and take their stand. I find a great many professed Christians for a long time have been ashamed to acknowledge that they have been spiritually awakened. Some have said that they did not like the idea of asking Christians to rise, as I did last evening; that it was putting them in a false position. Now, if we are going to be successful, we have to take our stand for God, and let the world and everyone know we are on the Lord's side. I have great respect for the woman who started out during the war with a poker. She heard the enemy was coming and went to resist him. When someone asked her what she could do with the poker, she said she would at least let people know which side she was on. That is just what we want. The time is coming when the line must be drawn in this city, and those on Christ's side must take their stand; and the moment we come out boldly and acknowledge Christ, then men will begin to inquire what they must do to be saved.

Then there is a class of people who are not warm enough. I do not think a little enthusiasm would hurt the Church at the present time. I rather think we need it. I know the world will cry out against it. Businessmen will cry out against religious enthusiasm. Let railway stocks go up fifteen or twenty percent, and see what a revival there would be in business. If there should be a sudden advance in stocks, see if there would not be enthusiasm on the Exchange tomorrow. Let there be a sudden improvement in business, and see if there is not a good deal of enthusiasm in the street. We can have enthusiasm in business; we can have enthusiasm in politics, and no one complains of that. A man can have enthusiasm in everything else, but the moment that a little fire gets into the Church, people raise the cry, "Ah, enthusiasm – false excitement – I am afraid of it." I do not want false excitement, but I do think we want a little fire, a little holy enthusiasm.

But these men raise the cry, "Zeal without knowledge." I would much rather have zeal without knowledge than knowledge without zeal, and it will not hurt us to have a little more of this enthusiasm and zeal in the Lord's work. I saw more zeal when I was in Princeton (referring to the Princeton Revival) last Sunday than I have in many years. I was talking to the students there about their souls, and after I had been talking for some time, a number of young men gathered around me, and the moment one of them made a surrender and said, "Well, I will accept Christ," twentyfive hands were at once stretched out to shake hands with him. That is what we want – men that will rejoice to hear of the conversion of men.

Although I do not admire his ideas, I do admire the enthusiasm of that man Garibaldi. It is reported that when he marched toward Rome in 1867, he was arrested and thrown into prison, and he sat right down and wrote to his comrades, "If fifty Garibaldis are thrown into prison, let Rome be free." That is the spirit. Who is Garibaldi? That is nothing. "If fifty Garibaldis are thrown into prison, let Rome be free." That is what we want in the cause of Christ. We must work and not loitering.

Then the question of dignity comes up. We have to lay all that aside and be willing to be helpers. What difference does it make if we are hewers of wood or carriers of water while the Temple of God is being erected? Yes, let us have an enthusiasm in the Church of God. If we had it in a few of the churches in New York, I believe it would be like a resurrection. The people would say, "What has come over this man? He is not like the same man he was two months ago." We want to have them say, "The Son of God is dearer to us than our money. The Son of God is dearer to us than our families. The Son of God is dearer to us than our position in society." Let us do anything so that the work of God may go on, and when we are willing to do this, God will bless us.

It says in the Bible, One of your men puts to flight a thousand (Joshua 23:10). We have not many of that kind in our churches. I wish we had more of them. It also says, Two put ten thousand to flight (Deuteronomy 32:30). Now, if a few would lay hold of God in this way, see what a great army will be saved in this city in no time! But then we have to be men after God's own heart. We cannot be lukewarm; we have to be on fire with the cause of Christ. We need to have more of this enthusiasm that will carry us into the Lord's work. If there is to be a great revival in New York, it will not come by simply holding meetings in this hall. It has to be brought about by one and another going around and talking to their neighbors. There is not a skeptic, nor a drunkard, who cannot be reclaimed if we come with desire in our hearts. We must not go around professionally if we want to see any results.

There is a story told in history, from the ninth century, I believe, of a young man who came up with a small group of men to attack a king with a great army of three thousand. The young man had only five hundred, and the king sent a messenger to him, saying that he need not fear to surrender, for he would treat him mercifully. The young man called up one of his soldiers and said, "Take this dagger and drive it to your heart." The soldier took the dagger and drove it to his heart. Calling up another, he said to him, "Leap into yonder chasm," and the man leaped into the chasm. The young man then said to the messenger, "Go back and tell your king I have five hundred men like these. We will die, but we will never surrender. And tell your king another thing, that I will have him a chained prisoner in a few more hours." When the king heard this, he did not dare to meet them. His army fled before them like chaff before the wind, and in a very short time, the young man had the king in chains.

That is the kind of zeal we want. "We will die, but we will never surrender." We will work until Jesus comes, and then we will rise with Him. Oh, if men are willing to die for patriotism, why can they not have the same zeal for Christ? All that Abraham Lincoln had to do was to call for men, and how speedily they came! When he called for 600,000 men, how quickly they sprang up all over the nation! Are not souls worth more than this Republic? Are not souls worth more than this Government? Do we not want 600,000 men?

If 600 men would come forward whose hearts were right

redhot for the Son of God, we would see what mighty results would follow. *One chase a thousand, and two put ten thousand to flight* (Deuteronomy 32:30). During our war, the generals who were always on the defensive never succeeded. The successful generals were those who took the offensive.

Some of our churches think they are doing remarkably well if they keep up their numbers in membership, and others think that having thirty or forty conversions in a year is remarkable work. Some think it is enough to fill the places of those who have died and those who have wandered away during the past year. It seems to me that we ought to bring thousands and thousands to Christ. I say the time has come for us to carry on an aggressive warfare. There may be barriers in our path, but God can remove them. There may be a mountain in our way, but God can take us over the mountain. There may be difficulties in the way, but God can overcome them. Our God is above them all, and if the Church of God is ready to advance, all obstacles will be removed. No man sent by God ever failed, but self must be lost sight of. We must be willing to lay down our lives for the cause of Christ.

When I was going to Europe in 1867, my friend Mr. Stuart, of Philadelphia, said, "Be sure to be at the General Assembly in Edinburgh in June. I was there last year," said he, "and it did me a world of good." He said that a returned missionary from India was invited to speak to the General Assembly on the wants of India. This veteran missionary (the venerable Dr. Duff), after a brief address, told the pastors who were present to go home and encourage their churches to send young men to India to preach the gospel. He spoke with such earnestness that, after a while, he fainted, and they carried him from the hall. When he recovered, he asked where he was, and they told him the circumstances under which he had been brought there. "Yes," he said, "I was making a plea for India, and I did not quite finish my speech, did I?" After being told that he did not, he said, "Well, take me back and let me finish it." But they, said, "No, you will die in the attempt." "Well," said he, "I will die if I do not," and the old man asked again that they would allow him to finish his plea. When he was taken back, the whole congregation stood as one, and as they brought him onto the platform, with a trembling voice he said: "Fathers and mothers of Scotland, is it true that you will not let your sons go to India? I spent twentyfive years of my life there. I lost my health, and I have come back with sickness and shattered health. If it is true that we have no strong grandsons to go to India, I will pack up what I have and be off tomorrow, and I will let those heathens know that if I cannot live for them, I will die for them."

The world will say that the old man was enthusiastic. Well, that is just what we want. No doubt, that is what they said of the Son of God when He was down here. Oh, that God may baptize us tonight with the spirit of enthusiasm! Oh, that He may anoint us tonight with the Holy Spirit!

Let me speak to some of you older people. I see some with grey locks here who, I have no doubt, are saying, "I wish I was young again. I would love to help in this work. I would love to work for the Lord." When we went to London, there was an old woman, eightyfive years old, who came to the meetings and said she wanted to have a hand in the work. She was assigned to a district and called on all classes of people. She went to places where we would likely have been turned away, and she spoke to people about Christ. There were none that could resist her. When this old woman came to them and offered to pray for them, they all received her kindly – Catholics, Jews, Gentiles, everyone.

That is enthusiasm. That is what we want in New York. If you cannot give a day to this work, give an hour; if not an hour, five minutes. If you have not the strength to do anything personally, you can pray for this work. It is far better to do that than to stand off criticizing. Some will say, "Oh, I heard my grandfather say how such things should be done. This is not being managed the right way to succeed." They stand off, criticize, and find fault. If everybody were like that, we would never succeed. Everyone should work and ask for God's guidance.

Once, when a great fire broke out at midnight and people thought that all the inmates had been taken out, way up in the fifth story of the house was seen a little child crying for help. A ladder went up and soon a fireman was seen ascending to the spot. As he neared the second story, the flames burst in fury from the windows, and the multitude almost despaired of the rescue of the child. The brave man faltered, but a comrade at the bottom cried out, "Cheer him!" and cheer upon cheer arose from the crowd. He went up the ladder and saved the child because they cheered him.

If you cannot go into the heat of the battle yourself, if you cannot go into the harvest field and work day after day, you can still cheer those who are laboring for the Master. I noticed that many old people, in their later years, become crusty and sour, discouraging everyone they meet with their faultfinding. That is not what we want. If we make a mistake, come and tell us about it, and we will thank you. You do not know how much you may do by just speaking kindly to those who are willing to work.

I remember when I was a boy, I went several miles from home with an elder brother. That seemed to me the longest visit of my life. It seemed that I was then farther away from home than I had ever been before, or have ever been since. While we were walking down the street, we saw an old man coming towards us, and my brother said, "There is a man who will give you a cent. He gives a cent to every new boy who comes into this town." That was my first visit to the town. When the old man reached us, he looked around. My brother, eager to ensure

I would not miss the cent and anxious to remind the old man that I had not received one yet, told him that I was a new boy in town. The old man, taking off my hat, placed his trembling hand on my head and told me that I had a Father in heaven. It was a kind, simple act, but I still feel the weight of the old man's hand upon my head today.

Now, you can all do something in this work of saving souls. That is what we have come to this city for. There is not a mother, father, wife, or young man in all the city who would not be in sympathy with this work. We have come here to try to save souls. I never heard of anyone who was injured by being brought to Christ. Oh, let us pray for the Spirit of God! Let us pray that the spirit of criticism and faultfinding may be all laid aside, and that we may be of one accord, as the disciples were on the day of Pentecost.

CHAPTER 4

TO EVERY MAN HIS WORK

It is like a man away on a journey, who upon leaving his house and putting his slaves in charge, assigning to each one his task, also commanded the doorkeeper to stay on the alert. – Mark 13:34

I want to call your attention to a passage you will find in the 13th chapter of Mark, part of the 34th verse – assigning to each one his task. Now, if you notice that verse carefully, it does not read "to each one some work," or "to each one a work," but "to each one his work." And I believe, if the truth were known, that every man and woman in this assembly has a work laid out for them to do; that every man's life is a plan of the Almighty, and that away back in the councils of eternity, God laid out a work for every one of us. There is no man living who can do the work that God has for me to do. No one can do it but myself. And if any man's work is not done, he will have to answer for it when he stands before the bar of God. For it is written: For we must all appear before the judgment seat of Christ, so that each one may be recompensed for his deeds in the body (2 Corinthians 5:10). And it seems to me that every one of us ought to take this question home tonight: "Well, am I doing the work that God has for me to do?" God has a work for every one of us to do.

Now, in the parable, the man with two talents received the same reward as the man with five talents, hearing the same approving words as the latter: Well done, good and faithful slave, ... enter into the joy of your master (Matthew 25:21, 23). If men take good care of the talents that God has lent to them, He always gives them more. But if we take the talent that God has given us and lay it carefully in a napkin and bury it, God will take even that from us. God does not expect a man who has but one talent to do the work of a man who has ten. All that a man has to answer for is for the talent or talents that God has given him. If we were all doing the work that God has for us to do, do you not see how the work of the Lord would advance? I believe in what John Wesley used to say, "All at it, and always at it," and that is what the Church wants today.

But men say, "I do not believe in these revivals; they are only temporary, they only last a short time." Ah, if I thought a revival was only to last a short time, I would say "Amen" to everything they say. For years, my prayer has been that God will let me die when the spirit of revival dies out of my heart, and I do not want to live any longer if I cannot be used to some purpose. What are we doing in this world of sickness and sorrow, unless it is to work for the Son of God, and improve the talents He has given us? Some men are not satisfied with the talents they have, but are always wishing for the talents of someone else. Now that is all wrong. It is contrary to the spirit of Christ. Instead of wishing for the talents of someone else, let us make the best use of those which God has given us.

There is not a father or a mother here but would think it a great misfortune if their children would not grow a bit for the next ten or fifteen years. If that little boy there would not grow at all for ten or fifteen years, his mother would say, "It is a great calamity." There are some men of my acquaintance who make the same prayers they made fifteen or twenty years ago. They are like a horse in a treadmill, going round and round – it is always the same old story of their experiences when they were converted.

If you had a child that was deaf and dumb, you would consider it a great misfortune. Do you ever think how many dumb children God has? You speak about political matters, and they can talk. You ask them what they think about General Grant's third term (referring to the then pending presidential election), and hear them talk! You ask them about stocks and bonds, and hear them talk! You speak to them about the hard times in New York, and see if they cannot talk. But ask them to speak about the Son of God, and they say: "Oh no, I cannot speak about that. Please excuse me." Either they do not believe, or they have gone like the third man and buried their talent, and they say, "The Lord is a hard master."

I remember a party of gentlemen once speaking of this parable that I read, and one of them asked a deaf man, "What do you think of this man hiding his talent, and about the justice of his reward?" The deaf man replied, "I do not know anything about the justice of his reward, but I know he is a liar. The Lord is not a hard master. He told lies when he said that." And so those men who bury their talents think the Lord is a hard master, but the men who are using their talents do not think the Lord is a hard master.

Let us do all the work we can. If we cannot be a lighthouse, let us be a tallow candle. There used to be a period when the people came up to meeting, bringing their candles with them. Certainly, the first one would not make a great illumination, but when two or three had arrived, there would be more light. If the people of this city would do that now, if each one would come here with his candle, do you not think there would be a little light? Let all the gas be put out in this hall, even one solitary candle would give some light here. If we cannot be a lighthouse, let us be a tallow candle. Someone said, "I cannot be anything more than a very small candle." Well, if you cannot be more, be that; that is well enough. Be all you can.

Why is it that many Christians are cold? Because they are all the time receiving, never giving out anything. You go every Sunday and hear good sermons, and think that is enough.

You are always receiving these grand truths, but never give them out. When you hear it, go and scatter the sacred truth abroad. Instead of having one minister to preach to a thousand people, this thousand ought to take a sermon, and spread it till it reaches those who never go to church or chapel. Instead of having a few, we would have thousands using the precious talents that God has given them.

We are told how Andrew, Simon Peter's brother, brought Peter to Christ. He went about it in the right way; he began right. Andrew inquired of the people, "Have you seen Peter anywhere?" and when he found him, he brought him to Jesus. Little did Andrew know of the importance of the day when he brought Peter to Christ. Little did he think that on that day, he did the greatest act of his life. What joy must have filled his heart when he saw three thousand brought under the influence of the Spirit by his brother's preaching. Oh, you cannot tell what results will follow if you just improve the talent God has given you by bringing one Simon Peter to Christ.

Later, when the Greeks came seeking Jesus, Andrew, along with his brother, Philip, brought them to Christ. Andrew rejoiced in bringing sinners to the Savior. I would rather be known for bringing sinners to Jesus than for any other. Oh, the joy there is in bringing people to Christ! This is what we all can do if we will. If God has given us but half a talent, let us make good use of that. He will give us just as many talents as we can take care of.

There are many of us who are willing to do great things for the Lord, but few of us are willing to do little things. The mighty sermon on regeneration was preached to one man (John 3). There are many who are willing to preach to thousands but are not willing to take their seat beside one soul, and lead that soul to the blessed Jesus. We must get down to personal effort – bringing one by one to the Son of God. We can find no better example of this than in the life of Christ Himself. Look at that wonderful sermon that He preached to that lone woman at the well of Samaria. He was tired and weary, but He had time and the heart to preach to her. This is but one of the many instances in the life of the Master from which we may learn a precious lesson. If the Son of God had time to preach to one soul, cannot every one of us go and do the same?

If people, instead of coming to these meetings, folding up their arms, and enjoying themselves without personal effort, would wake up to the fact that they have a work to do, imagine the wonderful work that could be done! It is not enough to come to these meetings; we want ten thousand workers in New York City. We want ten thousand men and women who are willing to say, "Lord, here am I, use me." Ten thousand of such people would revolutionize this city in no time. Look at the work of the mighty Wesley. The world never saw a hundred such men living at the same time.

The trouble is – we are afraid to speak to men about their souls. Let us ask God to give us grace to overcome this man-fearing spirit. There is a wife, but she dares not speak to her husband about his soul. There is a father who dares not speak to a son about his soul. What we ought to do is to speak to our neighbors about these things. We call it a little work, but let me say to you, it is a great work. If we would do this, we might turn ten thousand to the Son of God.

I remember hearing of a person who was always trying to do some great thing for the Lord, and because he could not do some great thing, he never did anything. There are a great many who would be willing to do great things if they could come up and have their names heralded through the press. I remember hearing of a man's dream in which he imagined that, when he died, he was taken by the angels to a beautiful temple. After admiring it for a time, he noticed that one stone was missing. Everything else was finished, but just one little stone was left out. He said to the angel, "What is this stone left out for?" The angel replied, "That was left out for you, but you wanted to do great things, and so there was no room left for you." He was startled and awoke, and resolved that he would become a worker for God. So the dream had a blessed result.

Now, my friends, we must not expect to do great things. We must take anything that comes to us. We must let the Lord use us as He sees fit. I remember once, while preaching at a meeting, I noticed a lady in the congregation who had a class in a mission school. I knew that it was the time for them to meet, and I wondered why she was there.

When I arrived home, I asked, "How did you happen to be at the meeting this afternoon? What did you do with all those little lambs? Don't you have a class that meets today?" "Yes," she replied, "but I only have five little boys, and I did not think it would matter if I did not teach them today." "You have five little boys?" "Yes." "How do you know but among those little boys there may be a Knox, or a Wesley, or a Whitefield, or a Bunyan? There may be a boy there who, when a man, will go out and revolutionize the world."

My friends, in that little boy with his tattered clothes and uncombed hair, there may be a Martin Luther, if you would but lead him to Christ. If you have five little children come to you, thank God for that, and start with your work.

I heard some time ago of a young lady who went away to a boarding school. Her parents were very wealthy and sent her to the best school they could find. They were very anxious that their daughter would shine in the highest circle of society, that she would become refined and educated. Among her associates at school was a lady who loved and worked for Christ. Through constant effort, she won this young girl's heart and pleaded with her to become a Christian. She succeeded, and the young lady became a worker in the vineyard of the Lord. She taught her the luxury of working for Christ. The young lady labored with her schoolmates, and God used her in winning quite a number in that school to Christ.

I have known a great many ministers who wanted to know how they could keep their congregation out of the world. Give them so much to do that they will not have time to cherish worldly associations. This young lady of whom I was speaking came home, and her father and mother wanted her to shine in fashionable society. "No," she said; she had learned something better than that. She went to the Sunday school superintendent, and said to him, "Can you give me a class in the Sunday school?" He was surprised that this young lady would want that. He told her he had no class he could give her then. She went away with a resolve to do what she could outside the school.

One day, as she was walking up the street, she saw a little boy running out of a shoemaker's shop, and behind him was the old shoemaker chasing him with a wooden shoe form in his hand. He had not run far before the shoe form was thrown at him, and he was struck in the back. The boy stopped and began to cry. The Spirit of the Lord touched that young lady's heart, and she went to where he was. She stepped up to him and asked him if he was hurt. He told her it was none of her business. She went to work then to win that boy's confidence.

She asked him if he went to school. "No," he answered. "Well, why don't you go to school?" "Don't want to," he replied. She then asked him if he would not like to go to a Sunday school. "If you will come," she said, "I will tell you beautiful stories and read nice books." She coaxed and pleaded with him, and at last said that if he would consent to go, she would meet him at the corner of a street which they would agree upon. The little boy finally consented.

The next Sunday, true to his promise, he waited for her at the place designated. She took him by the hand and led him into the Sunday school. "Can you give me a place in which to teach this little boy?" she asked of the superintendent. He looked at the lad, but they had no such boys like him in the school. A place was found, however, and she sat down in the corner and tried to win that soul for Christ. Many would look upon that effort with contempt, but she felt she had something to do for the Master. The little boy had never heard anybody sing so sweetly before.

When he went home, he was asked where he had been. "Been among the angels," he told his mother. He said that he had been to the Protestant Sunday school. His father and mother told him he must not go there anymore, or he would get a flogging. The next Sunday, he went again and, upon returning home, received the promised flogging. He went a second time and was flogged once more. A third time, he went, and the result was the same. At last, he said to his father, "I wish you would flog me before I go, so I won't have to think of it when I am there." The father said, "If you go to that Sunday school again, I will kill you." It was the father's custom to send his son out in the street to sell articles to the passersby, and he told the boy that he could keep the profits from what he sold on Saturdays. The little fellow hastened to the young lady's house and said to her, "Father said that he would give me every Saturday to myself, and if you will just teach me then, I will come to your house every Saturday afternoon."

I wonder how many young ladies there are who would give up their Saturday afternoons just to lead one boy into the kingdom of God! Every Saturday afternoon, that little boy was there at her house, and she tried to tell him the way to Christ. She labored with him, and at last, the light of God's Spirit broke upon his heart. One day, while he was selling his wares at the railroad station, a train of cars approached unnoticed and passed over both his legs. A physician was summoned, and the little sufferer looked up into his face the first thing after he arrived, asking, "Doctor, will I live to get home?" "No," said the doctor, "you are dying." "Will you tell my mother and father that I died a Christian?" They bore home the boy's corpse, and with it the last message – that he died a Christian. Oh, what a noble work was that young lady's in saving that little wanderer! How precious the remembrance to her! When she goes to heaven, she will not be a stranger there. That boy will be there to take her by the hand and lead her to the throne of Christ. She did the work cheerfully. Oh, may God teach us what our work is, that we may do it for His glory!

The greatest pleasure of living is to win souls to Christ, and it is a pleasure that angels cannot enjoy. It is sometimes a wonder to me that God does not take the work away from the Church and give it to the angels. If the redeemed saints could cross the great gulf, I sometimes think they would rejoice in coming back here to have the privilege of leading one more soul to Christ. Is it not high time that the Church awoke from its midnight slumber? It is time for the work to commence, and when the Spirit of God revives us, will we not go and do it? Are there not five thousand Christians in this hall? And is there not someone among them who can lead a soul to Christ within the next week? If we work, what a great army can be brought in, if we are only faithful! I want to say to the Christians here that there is one rule I have followed which has helped me wonderfully. I made it a rule that I would not let a day pass without speaking to someone about their soul's salvation; and if they do not hear the gospel from the lips of others, there will be three hundred and sixtyfive in a year who will hear the gospel from my lips. There are five thousand Christians here tonight; cannot they say, "We will not let a day pass without speaking a word to someone about salvation."

At a place where we were holding meetings in the gasworks, there was a man who came to our very first meeting. He was very much interested and said, "I will try and see if I cannot lead some of the men in my shop to Christ." He began to talk with them. There were 175 men on the night watch, and when I left, they said that 25 out of the 175 had been converted. Every night at midnight – that is, the hour when they have what might be called their midnight dinner – they held a prayer meeting. When you and I are asleep at night, those young converts will be speaking and praying; and it looks now as if every man in those gasworks was going to be brought to Christ.

When we were in Belfast, there was a man who heard about leading souls to Christ. He began by talking to his wife, his servant, and his children. Just as we were leaving Belfast, they were very much interested but not converted. He broke up his home, left his business, and went to Dublin. One night, he came to me very joyous, and he said, "My wife has been converted." A little while after, he returned and said, "My younger son has been converted." Not long after that, he came again to say, "My eldest son has been converted." Now, the whole family is in the ark. And perhaps in all Belfast, there are few who work harder for the Lord than that whole family.

Look at this man's success: he found that his work was right there in his own household. If the fathers, mothers, sisters, wives, and brothers, will try to bring the members of their families to Christ, and cry, "O God, teach me what my work is," the Spirit of God will surely tell them what their work is. And when they are ready to go and do it, there will be thousands converted in this city. Oh, may the Spirit of the Lord come upon us tonight! May each one of us be taught by the Holy Spirit what our work is, and may we be ready to do it!

CHAPTER 5

LOVE AND SYMPATHY

If I speak with the tongues of men and of angels, but do not have love, I have become a noisy gong or a clanging cymbal. – 1 Corinthians 13:1

I want to follow up the subject we have had during the past week in the noon prayer meeting. We have had for our subject "Prayer." In these meetings, a good many of you will remember, we have had the subject "Work." Now we want to put the two together, "Prayer and Work." It is to pray and to work.

I am in hopes we will be ready next Sabbath to go to work with individuals. I am in hopes there will be thousands of Christians who will each be trying to lead some soul to Christ. Now there are two qualifications which we need in order to be successful fishermen of men, in order to be successful in winning souls to Christ. Some of you will remember I took the subjects, "Courage and Enthusiasm." I now want to take two others, "Love and Sympathy."

I want to call your attention to the 1st verse of the 13th chapter of Corinthians, where we read that, *if I speak with the tongues of men and of angels, but do not have love, I have become a noisy gong or a clanging cymbal,* and where we are further told that if we even give our bodies to be burned, and yet have not real love in our hearts, our work will go for nought. I want to call your attention to a passage in Titus: *But as for you, speak the things which are fitting for sound doctrine. Older men are to be temperate, dignified, sensible, sound in faith, in love, in perseverance* (Titus 2:1).

If love does not prompt all work, all work is for nought. If a man in the church is not sound in his faith, we draw our ecclesiastical sword, and cut his head right off; but he may not be sound in love, yet we do nothing in his case. The great want in our churches is the want of love in them. If we had more love, we would do better, for love begets love, just as hate begets hate. You often hear a man say that such and such a man is the meanest man in town. Now, the other man may have had no illfeeling toward the speaker, but if he hears of the remark, he begins to think badly of the one who abused him and soon learns to hate him. Now, if a man hears that another man loves him and has spoken well of him, his love will flow out. Christ tells us, *By this all men will know that you are My disciples, if you have love for one another* (John 13:35). This love will be the badge of the Christian, the badge by which all will know to whom he belongs, like the badges the ushers wear in this hall.

Without love, we are not really converted to God. When we are truly converted, we love all things and all men better than ever before. The morning I was converted, I went outside, and I fell in love with the bright sun shining over the earth. I never so loved the sun before. And when I heard the birds singing their sweet songs, I fell in love with the them too, much like the Scotch lassie who stood on the hills of her native land, breathing the sweet air, and when asked why she did it, said: "I love the Scotch air." If the church were filled with love, it could do so much more.

I am tired of the word "duty." Tired of hearing duty, duty,

duty. Men go to church because it is their duty. They go to the prayer meeting because it is their duty. You can never reach a man's heart if you talk to him because it is your duty. Suppose I told my wife I loved her because it was my duty – what would she say? Once every year, I go up to Massachusetts to visit my aged mother. Suppose the next time I visit, I tell her that I know she is old and living on borrowed time; that I knew she has always done a great deal for me, and that I come to see her every year because it is my duty. Do you not think she would say, "Well then, my son, you do not need to take the trouble to come again"?

Let us strike for a higher plane. God loved the world when it was full of sinners and those who broke His law. If He did so, cannot we do it, and love our fellow men? If the Savior could die for the world, cannot we work for it? The churches would soon be filled if outsiders could find that people in them loved them when they came; if the elders and deacons were glad to see them, and were ready to take them by the hand and welcome them. Such things would draw sinners. Actions like these speak louder than words. We do not want to talk of love and not show it in our deeds; we want something more than tonguelove.

If our hearts go out toward men and we love them, they will be drawn toward us and we will win them to Christ. We must win them to us first, and then we can win them to Christ. The last time I heard Dr. Arnold (of America) speak – he died soon afterwards – he used a homely illustration. He said, "Those of you who were brought up on a farm will understand it. When you have to wean a calf, you have to teach it how to drink. You take a bucket of milk, and then you put your fingers in the calf's mouth, and when he has got a good hold, you pull his nose right down into the milk. Then you slip your fingers out, and the calf begins drinking before he knows anything about it." "So," he continued, "you must get the people to love you, and then turn them over to Christ." We must be more loving ourselves and show the people that we love them.

In our city a few years ago, there was a little boy who went to one of the Mission Sunday schools. His father moved to another part of the city, about five miles away, and every Sunday, that boy came past thirty or forty Sunday schools to the one he attended. One Sunday, a lady who was out collecting scholars for a Sunday school met him and asked him why he went so far, past so many schools. "There are plenty of others," she said, "just as good." He replied, "They may be as good, but they are not so good for me." "Why not?" she asked. "Because they *love* a fellow over there," he answered. Ah, love won him. "Because they love a fellow over there!" How easy it is to reach people through love! Sunday school teachers should win the affections of their scholars if they wish to lead them to Christ. Those who are successful in winning the affections of men are successful in leading them to Christ.

In London, in 1872, one Sunday morning, a minister said to me, "I want you to notice that family there in one of the front seats; and when we go home I want to tell you their story." When we arrived home, I asked him for the story, and he said, "That whole family was won by a smile."

"Why," said I, "how was that?" "Well," said he, "as I was walking down a street one day, I saw a child at a window; she smiled, and I smiled, and we nodded. The second time, the same thing happened. I nodded, she nodded. It was not long before there was another child, and I had got into a habit of looking and nodding; pretty soon, the group grew, and at last, as I went by, a lady was with them. I did not know what to do. I did not want to nod to her, but I knew the children expected it, so I nodded to them all. And the mother saw I was a minister because I carried a Bible every Sunday morning. The children followed me the next Sunday and found out I was a minister.

They thought I was the greatest preacher they knew, and their parents must hear me." If a minister is kind to a child and gives him a pat on the head, the children think he is the greatest preacher in the world. Kindness goes a long way. "And to make a long story short, the father and mother and five children were converted, and they are going to join our church next Sunday." *Won to Christ by a smile.*

We must get the wrinkles out of our brows, and we must have smiling faces. The world is after the best thing, and we must show them that we have something better than they have. I thought last night how I wished I knew the young men better. I have something better than infidelity. We must convince them of this, or those that live out of Christ will stumble over us into the lost world. Men are after the best thing everywhere, and we must show the world that we have the best thing before we win the world. If a man is after a horse, he wants to get the best horse he can for the money. If a lady goes shopping, she wants to get the best ribbon she can for the money. If a man wants a coat, he wants to get the best coat he can for the money. This is the law the world around. If we show men that religion is better than anything else, we will win the world; but we cannot do it if we are cold or lukewarm, and under the reproaches of conscience all the time.

We will not win the world to Christ if we are cold or lukewarm; but if the love of God beats in warm pulsations in our hearts, and we show them that we are full of love and sympathy for them, how easy it will be to win souls to Christ! I like to see in a Christian's face the light that comes down from the celestial hills of glory. Loving those that abused Him – that is what the Master did; and if we have His Spirit, we will certainly love those who do not love us. I do not think there is a man in New York whose heart is so hard that love cannot break it.

A friend of mine, who ran a large Sunday school, had a

theory that he would never turn a boy out of the Sunday school on account of bad conduct. "I considered," said he, "that those boys who behaved badly in the Sunday school had not had the advantages of a good bringingup, and for that very reason, they would not be turned away."

He soon realized, however, that it was one thing to have a theory and another to put it in practice. For he had a boy come into his Sunday school who nearly upset all his theory. He placed him under one teacher, but nothing could be done with him. He moved him to another teacher, but again, nothing worked. He eventually made up his mind to expel the boy publicly and let the whole school know about it. But there came a lady teacher to him who said: "I wish you would let me have that boy." "But," he said, "he is such a bad boy; he uses such bad language. None of those men can do anything with him, and I am nearly sure you cannot." The lady said, "I am not doing much for Christ, and it may be that I can win him." But she was a lady accustomed to refined society, and he thought, "Surely she will not have patience with that boy." He gave her the boy, and for a few Sundays, he behaved very well. But one Sunday, he behaved badly, and she corrected him, and he spat in her face. She quietly took her handkerchief and wiped her face. I do not know what his name was, but we will call him Johnny.

"Johnny," she said, "I wish you would go home with me. I want to talk with you." "Well, I won't," he replied, "I won't be seen in the street with you; and what's more, I ain't never coming to this Sunday school anymore." "Well," she said, "if you won't walk home with me, let me walk home with you." "No," he responded, "I would not be seen in the street with you, and I'm not coming to that dirty old Sunday school anymore."

She knew if she was going to reach that boy, it had to be then, so she decided to try. She thought she would just bear on the curiosity chord. Sometimes, when you cannot reach people in any other way, you do it by exciting their curiosity. She told him, "If you will come to my house next Tuesday morning, I will not be there; but if you will go there and ring the front doorbell and tell the servant there is a little bundle on the bureau for you, she will give it you."

The little fellow said he would not come. She fancied he might change his mind. He thought it over, and fancied he would just like to know what there was in that bundle. He went up to the house that Tuesday morning, and the bundle was handed to him. Inside, there was a little vest, a little necktie she had made with her own hands, and a kind note stating that ever since he had been in her class, she had been praying for him every morning and every evening. She also told him how much she loved and cared for him.

The next morning, he was at her door, bright and early, before she had even risen. The servant came up and told her that the boy was in the drawing room and wanted to see her. She went down and found the little fellow sitting on the sofa, weeping. She spoke to him kindly and asked, "What is your trouble?" and he said, "Oh, teacher, I have had no peace since I got that note from you." She knelt down and prayed with him. "And now," said the superintendent, "there is not a better boy in the school." *Love had conquered him.*

The greatest infidel can be reached by love. The greatest drunkard can be reached by love. Infidelity knows nothing about love. The religion of Jesus Christ is a religion of love. If we would be successful workers in His vineyard, it is the love of Christ that must bind us together. A few years ago, I was in a town down in our state, the guest of a family that had a little boy about thirteen years who did not bear the family name yet was treated like the rest.

Every night, when he retired, the lady of the house kissed him and treated him in every respect like all the other children.

I asked her, "I do not understand it." She answered, "I want to tell you about that boy. That boy is the son of a missionary. His father and mother were missionaries in India, but they found they had to send their children back to this country to be educated. So they left their mission field and came back to educate their children, and to seek some opening for Christian work in this country. But they were not prospered here as they had been in India. The father said, 'I will go back to India,' and the mother replied, 'If God has called you to go, I am sure it will be my duty to go and my privilege to go, and I will go with you.' The father said, 'You have never been separated from the children, and it will be hard for you to be separated from them; perhaps you had better stay and take care of them.'" After prayer, they decided to leave their children to be educated, and they left for India.

This lady heard of it and sent a letter to the parents, in which she stated that if they left one child at her house, she would treat that child like one of her own children. The mother came and spent a few days with her, and being satisfied that her boy would receive proper care, consented to leave him. The night before she was to leave him, the missionary's wife said to the Western lady: "I want to leave my boy tomorrow morning without a tear, for I may never see him again." But she did not want him to think she was weeping for anything she was doing for the Master. The lady thought to herself, "She will not leave that boy without a tear." But the next day when the carriage drove up to the door, the lady went upstairs and heard the mother in prayer, crying, "O God, give me strength for this hour. Help me to go away from my boy without a tear." When she came down, there was a settled calm upon her face. She embraced the lad and kissed him, without one outward sign of sorrow. She gave up all her five or six children without shedding a tear, went back to India, and in about a year, there came a voice, "Come up here."

Do you think she would be a stranger in the Lord's world? Do you not think she will be known there as a mother who loved her God more than her children? When I think of that mother, it seems as if I did not know much about making a sacrifice for my Master. Oh, that we might know more about the love of Christ!

The next thing I want to speak of is *sympathy*. We have to get into sympathy with people if we are going to do them good. This world wants sympathy as much as it wants anything. There are so many we could reach if we could sympathize with them. If we stand upon a higher plane than they, we will not succeed. The Son of God passed by the mansions and went down into a manger, that He might sympathize with the lowly. If we want to reach people, we have to put ourselves in the places of those people, if we are going to succeed. People say, "How are the masses to be reached?" Why, get into sympathy with them. If a man knows you are in sympathy with him, his heart, however hard it may be, will be broken.

A gentleman one day came to my office for the purpose of getting me interested in a young man who had just come out of the penitentiary. "He says," observed the gentleman, "he does not want to come and see you, but I want your permission to bring him in and introduce him." I said, "Bring him in." The gentleman brought him in and introduced him, and I took him by the hand and told him I was glad to see him. I invited him up to my house, and when I took him into my family, I introduced him as my friend. When my little daughter came into the room, I said, "Emma, this is papa's friend." She went up and kissed him, and the man sobbed aloud. After the child left the room, I said, "What is the matter?" "Oh, sir," he said,

"I have not had a kiss for years. The last kiss I had was from my mother when she was dying. I thought I would never love anyone again." His heart was broken. Just that little kindness showed I was in sympathy with him.

Another young man, just out of the penitentiary, came to me, and after I had talked with him for some time, he did not seem to think I was in sympathy with him. I offered him a little money. "No," he said, "I do not want your money." "What do you want?" "I want someone to have confidence in me." I knelt down and prayed with him; in my prayer, I called him a brother, and he shed tears the moment I called him a brother. So if we are going to reach men, we must make them believe we are their brethren. I will tell you how to reach men. You must put yourselves in their places. I tell you, if we only put ourselves in their places, we can succeed in bringing souls to Christ. When we see a poor drunkard, let us bear in mind that we might have been in the same place under the same circumstances.

Oh, may God give us love and sympathy, so that we can reach the masses! And oh, that we may see men coming to Christ by thousands! Let every one of us that love the Lord Jesus Christ make up our minds that, by the grace of God, we will try to help some soul to Christ; and the Lord will make us wise in leading souls to Him, if that is our prayer.

CHAPTER 6

THE GOSPEL

The Spirit of the Lord is upon Me, because He anointed Me to preach the Gospel to the poor.
– Luke 4:18

I want to call your attention to a verse in the 4th chapter of the Gospel of Luke: *The Spirit of the Lord is upon Me, because He anointed Me to preach the Gospel to the poor.* I have spoken a great many times in New York City, but I believe I never preached the gospel here but once. That was twelve or fifteen years ago, down at "The Tombs" ("The Tombs" is the New York City Prison). I have spoken a great many times in different parts of the city, but I have never preached the gospel but once. I have tried to arouse Christians to work. People are in the habit of thinking that anything in the way of a religious meeting is preaching the gospel, but they are mistaken. I have had quite a number of letters from Christians complaining because I do not preach the gospel to the people. I want to tell you, if I can, what the gospel of the Son of God is. I want to ask all those who are Christians here, to be silently lifting up their hearts in prayer that God may help me to make *the way of life* plain, and that everyone may know what the gospel of God is. I believe I was converted years before I knew what the gospel meant. Now the word "gospel" means "good spell," or, in other words, "God's spell."

When Christ commenced His ministry, almost His first words were, "The Spirit of the Lord is upon Me, because He anointed Me to preach the Gospel to the poor." That does not necessarily mean those who are poor in this world's goods, but it means the poor in spirit. Christ says, "The Lord hath anointed Me," for that purpose. He had been out of Nazareth for a few weeks and had gone down to Jordan, where He had met the great wilderness preacher. Christ had left Nazareth and went to meet John, that man from the desert, who was more like Elijah than any man since Elijah went up to heaven in a chariot of fire. There were gathered a great many people, tens of thousands of people probably, and John was crying that the kingdom of heaven was at hand. Among the audience came a Man who passed down into the water, and He requested John to baptize Him. John said that he needed to be baptized of Him. And after the baptism, there came a Voice – God confessed His Son: *This is My beloved Son, in whom I am well-pleased* (Matthew 3:17).

Those thousands took the tidings all over the country, and the news had reached Nazareth that Christ had been baptized by John, in Jordan, and that there came down a Voice from Heaven, saying, This is My beloved Son. When He arrived in Nazareth, there was no small assemblage ready to meet Him. He went into the synagogue, as was His custom, and He stood up and read the prophecy of the prophet Isaiah. He unrolled the scroll to read – they did not have books to open and shut like ours; they had parchment scrolls. He might have unrolled to the first chapter, and might have read, But Israel does not know, My people do not understand. Or He might have read, From the sole of the foot even to the head there is nothing sound in it. He passed by the

35th chapter—then the eyes of the blind will be opened and the ears of the deaf will be unstopped. He might have read that, but Calvary had to witness a victory before that could be fulfilled. He passed over the 9th chapter; he passed over the 40th chapter. He might have turned to the 55th chapter. He had not been wounded. He had not yet gone through Gethsemane.

But we read that He found the place where it is written, The Spirit of the Lord God is upon me, because the Lord has anointed me to bring good news to the afflicted (Isaiah 61:1). In Luke's Gospel, we have it rendered, He anointed Me to preach the Gospel to the poor. And that was the commencement of His ministry, and that was on His going back to Nazareth. And in that 61st chapter of Isaiah, He stopped right in the middle of a sentence. There were seven things He had come to do. He read the part that told that He had come to preach the gospel to the poor. The next was, *He has sent me to bind up the brokenhearted*. Was not that good tidings? You would think that was good tidings, would you not? The next was, He had come to proclaim liberty to the captives, followed by the recovering of sight to the blind, to set at liberty them that are bruised, and to proclaim the acceptable year of the Lord. Then He roll the scroll close. And the eyes of the whole congregation were upon Him.

The next sentence, the sentence which He omitted and did not read, was, *The day of vengeance of our God*. I have an idea that when the prophet Isaiah wrote those words, he did not fully see the first and second comings of Christ. That first coming has long since passed, but "the day of vengeance" has not yet come. So it seems as if the Prophet Isaiah did not understand the distinction between the first and second comings of our Lord.

Christ closed the scroll. He will return by and by, and He will open the scroll, and will commence to read where He left off. You may cry for mercy then, but the door will be shut.

But Christ did not then come to condemn sinners. He came

to save them. I have not come to New York to preach, "The day of vengeance is at hand." I have come to proclaim the gospel of Jesus Christ. I have come to tell you the good tidings: Christ did not come into the world to condemn the world, but that through Him the world might be saved. In the 9th chapter of Luke, you will read that He called His twelve disciples together and gave them power and authority over devils, and to heal the sick; that is what He came for – to preach the gospel of God and to heal the sick. Then in the next chapter, He calls around Him the seventy. He had appointed other seventy also – and He sent them, two and two, before His face into every city and place where He Himself would come.

Now, we find that He had come into the world just to bring glad tidings. Did you ever see or hear of anyone that did not like to receive glad tidings? One proof that people do not believe the Bible is when they wear long faces, as if they had accepted an invitation to an execution. That is not the gospel. The gospel is good news of great joy which will be for all the people; for today in the city of David there has been born for you a Savior, who is Christ the Lord (Luke 2:10,11). Better news never fell upon the ears of mortal man than the news of the gospel. I do not believe any man ever heard better tidings; they are glad tidings of heaven.

God had but one Son, and He sent Him to tell that good news: *The Spirit of the Lord is upon Me, because He hath anointed Me to preach the gospel to the poor.* We find that Moses was anointed. He went down into Egypt, and death followed. When he was opposed, look at the plagues that fell upon the Egyptians. We find that the Spirit of God was upon Elijah. When he wanted to protect himself, men lost their lives. Those two troops, each of fifty men, came to fetch Elijah (2 Kings 1), and he called fire down from heaven; and at the end of his course, he was taken up to heaven. The Spirit of God came down upon

Gideon, and when men came out to meet him, he killed them by thousands. The Spirit of God came upon Samson, and he killed men by thousands. The Spirit came upon those mighty men of old. But when Christ came, He said, *"*The Spirit of the Lord is upon Me" – not to take men's lives, but to save them. The only man who lost anything was the man who lost his ear, and that was not for long. Peter's faith became lukewarm, and he cut off a servant's ear, but the Lord gave it back to him. I do not suppose he lost it for more than five minutes, and it was just as good as ever when he had it back. I do not suppose you could find a scar there.

Christ said, *the Son of Man did not come to destroy men's lives, but to save them* (Luke 9:56). It seems to me to be the greatest madness that the world does not receive Christ. Is it not a mystery that we would have to coax and entreat men to receive Christ? Suppose that, while I am preaching, a messenger would come in and bring in a letter that conveyed good tidings to some mother here? Do you not believe she would be glad to receive it? Suppose it told her that her boy, who has been away for ten years, had returned. He ran away ten years ago, and the messenger comes in and states that the runaway has come home. Do you not think that mother's face would light up? I would see her joy in her countenance. And so, when I preach the gospel, I cannot but know by their faces those that believe. Gladness lights up their faces. Look at our churches, how the people throng to them to hear the gospel. Let a man preach about something else than the gospel and see if the people would throng to them. There is a void in every one's heart that will never be filled until the gospel of Christ is received.

Now, I want to tell you why I like the gospel, for I do not believe God calls on us to believe the gospel without giving us good reason for it; and I do not believe He would call it good news unless He gave us good reason for it. Now, it has taken out of my path four of the most bitter enemies I had. The 15th chapter of 1 Corinthians tells us that *the last enemy that will be abolished is death*. I see by the badges of mourning among you that many of you have lost loved ones. Many of you know what it is to have death come to your door when some loved child has been taken from your bosom. Possibly some of you will say, "If a person is afraid of death, he is a coward." I do not believe any man or woman ever lived who was not afraid of death, unless they knew that Jesus Christ would overcome death. Before I knew the Son of God as my Savior, death was a terrible enemy to me.

Up in that little New England village from which I came, it was the custom to toll the bell whenever anyone died, and to toll one stroke for every year. Sometimes they would toll seventy strokes for a man of seventy, or forty strokes for a man of forty. I used to think when they died at seventy, and sometimes at eighty, "Well, that is a good way off." But sometimes it would be a child at my age, and then it used to be very solemn. Sometimes I could not bear to sleep in a room alone. Death used to trouble me, but, thanks be to God, it does not trouble me now. If He would send His messenger, and the messenger would come up here on this platform and say to me, "Mr. Moody, your hour is come; I have to take you away," it would be joyful news for me; for though I would be absent from the body, I would be present with the Lord. Throughout the world I can shout, "O death, where is your sting?" That is what Calvary means. The wages of sin is death, but He took the wages Himself. That is the gospel of the Son of God, and there is no fear for those who believe in Christ Jesus. There was Paul; he had virtually triumphed over death. Let death come – "O death, where is your sting?" Sometimes I used to go into a graveyard when someone was about to lie down in that narrow house, and when the gravedigger shoveled and threw in the earth upon the coffin, it would be like a death knell to my soul. I could hear him say, "Ashes to ashes, dust to dust." Now I can measure its depths. I can shout, as Paul did, "O death, where is your sting?" This soul of man will go into the house not made with hands, eternal in the heavens. Oh, the grave is lost in victory. It is lost in Christ.

Oh, the blessed gospel of the Son of God! What could we do without it? When we lay our little children away in death, they will rise again. I was going into a cemetery once, and over the entrance I saw these words: "They shall rise again." Infidelity did not teach that; we learned that from this Book. Oh, the blessed gospel of the Son of God! How every one of you would believe it! Young lady, if you have been careless up to this afternoon, oh, may you wake up! May you, this hour, decide to turn from your sins unto God, and believe the gospel of His Son! I used to be a good deal troubled with my sins, and I thought of the Day of Judgment, when all the sins that I had committed in secret would blaze out before the assembled universe. But when a man comes to Christ, the gospel tells him they are all gone, and in Jesus Christ, he is a new creature. All I know is that because of the love which my Lord has for me, He has taken all my sins and cast them behind His back. That is, behind God's back. How is Satan to get at them? If God has forgiven our sins, they will not be mentioned. In Ezekiel, we are told not one of them will be mentioned (Ezekiel 18:22; 33:16). Is it not a glorious thing to have all our sins blotted out?

And there is another thought – and that is the Judgment. If a man has committed some great crime, you know how he dreads being brought to judgment. How he dreads that day when he is to be brought into court, when he is to be put into a box, and witnesses are to come up and testify against him, and he is there to be judged! But, my friends, the gospel tells us that if we come to Christ, we will never come into judgment.

Why? Because Christ was judged for us. *He was wounded for our transgressions* (Isaiah 3:5, KJV). If He has been wounded for us, we have not to be wounded. "Verily, verily," – which means truly, truly – *I say to you* – now just put your name in there – *He who hears My word, and believes Him who sent Me* – has, has. It does not say you *will have* when you die. It says, has – *He who hears My word, and believes Him who sent Me, has eternal life, and does not come into judgment* (John 5:24). He will not come into judgment, but *has passed out of death into life*. There is judgment out of the way. He will never come into judgment. Why? Because God has forgiven us, and given us eternal life. That is the gospel of Jesus Christ. Ought people to be gloomy and put on long faces when that is the news?

Away on the frontier of our country, out on the prairies, where men go to hunt or for other purposes, the grass in the dry seasons sometimes catches fire, and you will see the flames rise up twenty or thirty feet high. You will see those flames rolling over the Western desert faster than any fleet horse can run. Now, what do the men do? They know it is sure death unless they can make their escape. They would try to hurry away perhaps, if they had fleet horses. But they cannot; that fire goes faster than the fleetest horse can run. What do they do? Why, they just take a match, and they light the grass with it, and away it burns. Then they get into that burnt district. The fire comes on, and there they stand perfectly secure. There they stand perfectly secure – nothing to fear. Why? Because the fire has burned all there is to burn. Take your stand there on Mount Calvary.

The gospel of Jesus Christ is to "whosoever" will come. I thank God that I can come to this city of New York with a gospel that is free to all. It is free to the most abandoned. It may be there are some wives that have become discouraged and disheartened. I can tell you the joyful news that your husbands and your sons have not gone so far but that the grace of God can save them. The Son of God came to raise up the most abandoned.

On my way down here this morning, I noticed not less than four or five tramps. They looked weary and tired. I suppose they had slept on the sidewalk last night. I thought I would have liked to have had time just to stop and tell them about the Son of God, and how Christ loved them. The gospel of the Son of God is to tell us how He loves us. He takes our feet out of the pit, and He plants them on the Rock of Ages. And that, my dear friends, is what Christ wants to do. There is not a soul in any one of your homes but what He wants to save. Tell them there is none so abandoned, none so old, none so fallen, but that God can save them. There was Whitefield; and the Spirit of the Lord was upon him, and he said, "God is so anxious to save souls that He will take the devil's castaways." Whitefield said that the Lord would take the devil's castaways. There was William Dawson, the Yorkshire farmer – they used to call him "Billy Dawson." The power of the Lord was upon him, and in closing his meeting one night, he said there was not a man in London so far gone but that the Lord could save him.

There was a lady who found a man who said there was no hope for him; he had sinned away his day of grace. She went to Dawson and said to him, "Mr. Dawson, will you go and see this man, and tell him what you said." Dawson said he would be glad to go and see him. He went up the stairs of a fivestory house, and away up in the garret where he found a young man lying upon some straw. He bent over him, whispered into his ear, and called him his friend. The young man looked startled. He said, "You are mistaken in the person when you say, 'My friend.' I have no friends. No one cares for me." Dawson told him that Christ was as much his friend as that of any man in London. Poor prodigal!

After he had talked with him for some time, he prayed with

him and read to him from the Bible. At last, the light of the gospel began to break in upon that darkened heart. This young man said to Mr. Dawson that he thought he would die happy if he knew his father was willing to forgive him. Dawson inquired of him, "Where does your father live?" The young man said he lived in the West End of London. Dawson said, "I will go and see him, and find out if he will not forgive you." But the young man resisted, saying, "No, I don't want you to do that. My father would abuse you if you would speak to him about me. He does not recognize me as his son now." Still, Mr. Dawson insisted, "I will go and see him."

He went to the West End of London, where he found a very fine mansion. A servant in livery came to the door and ushered him into the drawing room. Soon, the father, a bright, majestic-looking man, came into the room. Dawson held out his hand to shake hands with him, and said, "You have a son by the name of Joseph, have you not?" And when the father heard that, he refused to shake hands with him, and turned to leave the room. "If you have come up here to talk about that worthless vagabond," he said, "I want you to leave the house. He is no son of mine." Mr. Dawson replied, "He is yours now, but he won't be long; but he is yours now."

"Is Joseph sick?" the man asked. "Yes," said Dawson, "he is dying. I have not come for money. I will see that he has a decent burial. I have only come to ask you to forgive him." "Forgive him! forgive him!" exclaimed the father. "I would have forgiven him long ago if I had thought he wanted me to. Do you know where he is?" "Yes, sir, he is in the East End of London." "Can you take me to him?" "Yes, sir, I will take you to him."

The father ordered out his carriage and was soon on his way. When they arrived at the place, he said, "Did you find my boy here? Oh, if I had known he wanted me to, I would have taken him home long ago." When the father went into that room, he could hardly recognize his longlost boy. The father went over and kissed the boy, and said to him, "I would have forgiven you long, long ago, if I had known you wanted me to do so. Let me have you placed in the carriage, and I will take you home." But the boy said, "No, father, I am dying; but I can die happy in this garret, now that I know you are willing to forgive me." And he told his father how Jesus had received him. In a little while, he breathed his last, and out of that dark garret, he rose up into the kingdom of God.

Oh, my friends, there may be someone in New York who would rejoice to hear the gospel words. Oh, here is a Christian, shall he not publish them? And you that are not Christians, will you not come into the kingdom? Oh, that today you may receive Christ – this, I believe, is the prayer of hundreds who are gathered here.

CHAPTER 7

THE GOSPEL TO THE POOR

The Spirit of the Lord is upon Me, Because He anointed Me to preach the gospel to the poor.
– Luke 4:18

You that were here last night, remember I was speaking on the text: *The Spirit of the Lord is upon Me, Because He anointed Me to preach the gospel to the poor.* I want to continue the subject we had last night. We do not want to get over that word "gospel" too soon. It is too precious. And I do not know but that it would be well to preach the same thing over and over again here, until you believe it. I heard of a minister who preached the same sermon three times. Some of the brethren went to him and told him he better preach another sermon. He said that when his congregation believed that, he would preach another sermon, but he did not propose to do so until they did.

The Spirit of the Lord is upon Me, because He hath anointed Me to preach the Gospel. Now, the question is – To whom shall the gospel be preached? There is a certain class of people who seem to think the gospel is very good for drunkards and thieves and vagabonds; there are many selfrighteous Pharisees today who are drawing their filthy rags of selfrighteousness around them and thinking the Bible is for a certain class. If I understand the Bible correctly, the gospel is *for all*. We read in the last chapter of Mark – almost the last words the Son of God uttered on this earth were to his disciples: *Go into all the world and preach the gospel to all creation* (Mark 16:15). When we come to the gospel, there is no distinction; rich and poor must be served alike; learned and unlearned; all have to come into the kingdom of God one way, and that is by believing the gospel of Jesus Christ. Now these words were uttered after Christ had tasted death for every man. Gethsemane was now behind Him; Calvary, with all its horrors, was past. He was just ready to go home to take His seat at the right hand of the Father. He was just giving the disciples His parting message. In other words, He was giving them His commission to go into all the world and preach the gospel to every creature. *He who has believed and has been baptized shall be saved* (Mark 16:16).

I can just imagine all that little band of disciples who stood around Him, those unlearned men of Galilee, those fishermen who had been associated with Him for three years. I can imagine the tears trickling down their cheeks as He talked of leaving them, and one of them thinking that the Lord did not really mean that, that He did not mean that they should preach the gospel to every creature. For He had a hard time making them believe that the gospel should be preached to the Gentiles. It seemed as if the Jews wanted to keep the gospel in Palestine; but by the grace of God, it would flow out; it would go forth to the world, because He had given orders that the gospel should be preached to every creature.

And now we find the messengers are to go to the four corners of the earth to proclaim the glad tidings of the gospel of Christ. But I can imagine Peter saying: "Lord, You do not really mean that we should preach the gospel to those men who murdered you, to those men who took Your life." "Yes," says the Lord, "go and preach the gospel to those Jerusalem sinners." I can imagine Him saying: "Go and hunt up that man who put the cruel crown of thorns upon My brow and preach the gospel to him. Tell him he will have a crown in My kingdom without a thorn in it; that he may sit upon My throne if he will accept of salvation as a gift. Go hunt up that man that spat in My face and preach the gospel to him and offer him salvation and tell him he can be saved if he is only cleansed by the blood I have shed at Calvary. Go to the man that thrust the spear into My side, and tell him there is a way of salvation. Tell him there is nothing in My heart but love for him. Go preach the gospel *to every creature*."

And after He had gone up on high, we find the Holy Spirit came down on the tenth day, and then they began to preach. Now see Peter standing there on the day of Pentecost and preaching the gospel of God to sinners. John Bunyan says, "If a Jerusalem sinner can be saved there is hope for us all." Do you think God is mocking? Do you think God is preaching the gospel to you, and yet withholding from you the power to receive it? The gospel is preached *to every creature*. And do you think He is not willing that every creature on the face of the earth should be saved?

Now, I like to proclaim the gospel, because it is to be proclaimed *to all*. When I see a poor drunkard, when I see a thief, when I see a prisoner in yonder prison, it is a grand, glorious thing to go and proclaim to him the glad tidings, because I know he can be saved. There is not one who has gone so far or fallen so low that he cannot be saved, because every one of God's proclamations is headed "whosoever." That takes in everybody; nobody is left out. Somebody said he would rather read "whosoever" than see his own name, because he would be afraid it might refer to some other man who might have the same name.

This was well brought out in a prison the other day, when the chaplain said to me, "I want to describe a scene that occurred here some time ago. Our commissioners went to the governor of the state and got him to give his consent to grant pardons to five men on account of their good behavior. The governor said the record was to be kept secret; the men were to know nothing about it. At the end of six months, the criminals were brought out, the roll was called, and the president of the commission came up and spoke to them. Then, putting his hand in his pocket, he drew out the papers and said to those 1,100 convicts, 'I hold in my hand pardons for five men.' I never witnessed anything like it. Every man held his breath and was as silent as death. Then the commissioner went on to tell how they obtained these pardons; that it was the governor who granted them."

The chaplain said the suspense was so great that he spoke to the Commissioner and asked him to first read out the names of those who were pardoned before he spoke further. The first name was given out thus: "Reuben Johnson will come out and get his pardon." He held out the paper, but no one came. He looked all around, expecting to see a man spring forward at once; still, no one arose. He turned to the officer of the prison and said: "Are all the convicts here?" "Yes," was the reply. "Then, Reuben Johnson will come and get his pardon."

The real Reuben Johnson was all this time looking around to see where Reuben was, and the chaplain beckoned to him. He turned and looked around and behind him, thinking some other man must be meant. A second time, the chaplain beckoned to Reuben and called to him, and again the man looked around to see where Reuben was, until at last the chaplain said to him, "You are the man, Reuben." He rose up out of his seat and sank back again, thinking it could not be true. He had been there for nineteen years, having been placed there for life. When he came up and took his pardon, he could hardly believe his eyes. He went back to his seat and wept like a child. Then, when the convicts were marched back to their cells, Reuben, having been so long in the habit of falling into line and taking the lockstep with the rest, fell into his place, and the chaplain had to say, "Reuben, come out; you are a free man."

That is the way men obtain their pardons – for good behavior; but the gospel of Jesus Christ is offered to those who have not behaved well. It is offered to all who have sinned and are unworthy. All a man has to prove now is that he is not worthy, and I will show him that Christ died for him. Christ died for us while we were yet in sin.

When we were in London one day, Mr. Spurgeon took Mr. Sankey and me to his orphan asylum, and he was telling about the children – that some of them had aunts and some cousins, and that nearly every boy seemed to have some friend who took an interest in him, came to see him, and gave him a little pocket money. But he said that one day, while he was there, a little boy came up to him and said, "Mr. Spurgeon, let me speak to you." The boy sat down between Mr. Spurgeon and the elder who was with him and said, "Mr. Spurgeon, suppose your father and mother were dead, and you had no cousins, or aunts, or uncles, or friends to come and give you pocket money or presents, don't you think you would feel bad? – *because that's me!*" Mr. Spurgeon said, "The minute he said that, I put my right hand down into my pocket and took out some money for the child."

"*Because that's me!*" And so with the gospel; it is for sinners, and if any one of you present here can say, "*Because that's me!*" then the gospel is for you.

As I was talking last night in the inquiry room, a man tried to assure me that he had made many mistakes but had committed no sins. They were all "mistakes" instead of sins. Better call things by their right names. We have all sinned. There are none righteous in themselves, and there is no man who walks the streets who has not broken the law of God. Therefore, all need a Savior, and there is no chance of being saved, no hope of any man being saved, unless he will admit first that he has sinned and is lost. Of course, if a man has not sinned, he will not need a Savior; but it is just because we have sinned that we need the gospel. Now, as I stated last night, the gospel is the very best tidings that can come to us. Christ comes to bless us.

In Glasgow, they were telling me of a scene that occurred when Dr. Arnot was preaching there. A woman was in great distress about her rent. She could not pay it, and so he took some money, and went to the house. He went to the door and knocked. He listened and thought he heard the footsteps of someone inside, so he knocked louder. No one came, and he knocked still louder; but after waiting some time, he went away disappointed. A few days afterward, he met this woman outdoors and told her that he had heard she had been in great distress, and he had called at her residence with the purpose of helping her but could not gain admittance. She threw up both hands and said, "Why, Doctor, that was not you, was it? I was in the house all the time, and I thought it was the landlord coming for the rent, so I kept the door bolted."

Now, Christ comes to bless. He does not come to demand. He does not come to ask you to do something that you cannot do. He comes to bless you. When He commenced His Sermon on the Mount, what did He say? "Blessed! blessed! Blessed!" When He was ready to go back to heaven, He raised His hands over that little company and breathed blessings upon them. And so, my friends, He comes into this building tonight to bless you; to help you. He offers to be your salvation; He offers to pay all the debt you owe. You owe God a debt you cannot pay. Can you forget this? You have broken the law of God. What are you going to do with the sins you have committed?

What is your hope? There is no hope unless your sins are blotted out by the Lord Jesus, unless Christ pays the penalty. If Christ settles the claim, the claim is settled for all time. And that is the doctrine of the Bible, the glorious doctrine of substitution. Christ paid the penalty, Christ died in our stead.

There was a man converted in Europe several years ago, and he liked the gospel so well, he thought he would like to go and publish it. Well, he started out to publish it, and great crowds came to hear him out of curiosity, just as a great many come here out of curiosity, to hear the singing, or something of that kind. Well, they came to hear him. The man was not much of a speaker, so the next night there were not many there, and on the third night, the man scarcely had a hearer. But he was anxious to publish the gospel, and so he prepared some great placards and posted them all over the town, declaring that if there was any man in that town who was in debt and would come to his office between certain hours on a certain day with the proof of indebtedness, he would pay the debt. Well, of course this news spread all over the town, but the people did not believe him. One man said to his neighbor, "John, do you believe this man will pay our debts?" "Oh, of course not; it is only a hoax." The day came, and instead of there being a great rush, nobody came.

Now, it is a wonder that there is not a great rush of men into the Kingdom of God to have their debts paid, when a man can be saved for nothing.

About ten o'clock, there was a man walking in front of the office; he looked this way and that to see if there was anybody looking, and by and by, satisfied there was nobody looking, he slipped in, and said, "I saw a notice about town that if anyone would call here at a certain hour, you would pay their debts. Is there any truth in it?" "Yes," says the man, "it is quite true. Did you bring the necessary papers with you?" "Yes." And after the man had paid the debt, he said, "Sit down, I want to talk with you," and he kept him there until twelve o'clock. Before twelve o'clock had passed, two more came in and had their debts paid. At twelve o'clock, he let them all out, when they found some other men standing around the door, they said, "Well, you found he was willing to pay your debts, did you not?" "Yes," they said. It was quite true that he had paid their debts. "Oh, if this is so, we shall go in and get our debts paid." And they went in, but it was too late. The man said if they had called within certain hours, he would have paid their debts.

To every one of you that is a bankrupt sinner – and you never saw a sinner in the world who was not a bankrupt sinner – Christ comes, and He says, "I will pay the debt." And that is just what He wants to do tonight. Bear in mind that the Son of God came into the world to save sinners, and that He has the power to forgive sin. And He not only has the power, but He is willing to save, and He is anxious to save; and so, my friends, if you will accept Christ's offer, you can leave this Hall tonight cleansed of all sin.

Now the question comes, "Who will accept Him?" I can imagine some man down in the audience will say, "Well, I don't think a man can be saved so easy. I don't believe in these sudden conversions. I don't believe a man can come in here and be saved at once." What is it God has for us? Is it a gift? We read in Romans that it is a gift: *For the wages of sin is death, but the free gift of God is eternal life in Christ Jesus our Lord* (Romans 6:23). Now, if a man is saved, there must be one minute when he does not have the gift, and there must be another minute when he has it. And that is what is represented in the Bible. It is a gift. "Well," someone may say, "don't I have to feel something before I can be saved? How much have I to give up?" "Give up your sins!" No, you don't have to give them up, for if you just accept Christ, they will go of themselves. They will flee away in the dim past. But you cannot do it of yourself. For a long time, I tried in my own strength to give up my sins, and I could not do it. But the moment I accepted Christ, He snapped the cords, and I have been rejoicing for the last twenty years. And the way to be saved is not to delay, but to come and take – take, take.

When I was in Glasgow, a lady said to me, "You use that word 'take' very frequently. Is there anything of that kind in the Bible? I cannot find it." Why, in the Bible it says, *The Spirit and the bride say, "Come." And let the one who hears say, "Come." And let the one who is thirsty come; let the one who wishes take the water of life without cost* (Revelation 22:17). And if God says, "Let him take," He will supply him. If that boy will take Christ, who can stop him? All hell and all earth cannot stop him. If need be, God would send ten thousand legions of angels to help him on his way up.

I tell you, if you are not saved, it is because you do not want to be. *You are unwilling to come to Me so that you may have life* (John 5:40). The door hangs on that hinge. If a man says, "I will arise and go to Him," he will not be kept long waiting. When the prodigal returned, it was not when he had arrived home that the change took place. It was away, away off in that foreign country, when he said, "I will arise and go to my father." I think the turning point with men will be when they say, "I will come, for I want to." If you want to go to heaven, the first thing is to make up your mind to go. If I want to go to Chicago, the first thing I do is to make up my mind to go. And if you are willing to go to Christ, no power on earth can keep you away. Now, those men here who say they cannot come, just be honest and put in the right word, and say you will not come.

At one time, my sister had trouble with her little boy, and the father said, "Why, Sammy, you must go now and ask your mother's forgiveness." The little fellow said he would not. The father said, "You must. If you do not go and ask your mother's forgiveness, I will have to undress you and put you to bed."

He was a bright, active little fellow, never still a moment, and the father thought he would dread being undressed and put to bed. But the little fellow would not yield, so they undressed him and put him to bed.

The father went to his business, and when he came home at noon, he said to his wife, "Has Sammy asked your forgiveness?" "No," she said, "he has not." So the father went to him and said, "Sammy, why don't you ask your mother's forgiveness?" The little fellow shook his head, "Won't do it." "But, Sammy, you must." "Can't."

The father went down to his office and stayed all the afternoon there. When he came home, he asked his wife, "Has Sammy asked your forgiveness?" "No; I took something up to him, and tried to get him to eat but he would not." So the father went up to see him, and said, "Now, Sammy, just ask your mother's forgiveness, and you may be dressed and come down to supper with us." "Can't do it." The father coaxed, but the little fellow said "can't do it." That was all they could get out of him. You know very well that he could, but he did not want to. Now, the hardest thing a man has to do is to become a Christian, and it is the easiest. That may seem a contradiction, but it is not. The hard point is because he does not want to. The hardest thing for a man to do is to give up his will.

That night the father and mother retired, and they thought, "Surely, early in the morning the boy will be up and ready to ask his mother's forgiveness." The father went to him – that was Friday morning – to see if he was ready to ask his mother's forgiveness, but he "couldn't." The father and mother felt so grieved about it they could not eat; they thought this matter seemed likely to darken their whole life. Perhaps that boy thought that his father and mother did not love him. Just as many sinners think when God does not let them have their own way.

The father went to his business, and when he came home,

he said to his wife, "Has Sammy asked your forgiveness?" "No." So he went to the little fellow and said, "Now, Sammy, are you not going to ask your mother's forgiveness?" "Can't." And that was all they could get out of him. The father could not eat any dinner; it was like death in the house. It looked as if the boy was going to conquer his father and mother. Instead of his little will being broken, it seemed very much as if he was going to break theirs. Late on the Friday afternoon, "Mother, mother, forgive," says Sammy, "me." As the little fellow said, "Me," he sprang to his feet and said, "I have said it, I have said it. Now dress me, and take me down to see father. He will be so glad to know I have said it." And she took him down, and when the little fellow came into the room he cried out, "I've said it, I've said it."

Oh, my friends, it is so easy to say, "I will arise and go to my Father." It is the most reasonable thing you can do. Is it not an unreasonable thing to hold out? Come right to God just this very hour. *Believe in the Lord Jesus, and you will be saved* (Acts 16:31). And now, this night, believe, and you will be saved.

CHAPTER 8

YE MUST BE BORN AGAIN

Truly, truly, I say to you, unless one is born again he cannot see the kingdom of God. – John 3:3

I will direct your attention to John. Jesus answered and said to him, "Truly, truly, I say to you, unless one is born again he cannot see the kingdom of God" (John 3:3). You will see by the 3rd chapter of Romans that it is absolutely necessary that a man be born again. You can see in the 3rd chapter of Romans what man is by nature. If you want to find out what God is, turn to the 16th verse of the 3rd chapter of John: *For God so loved the world, that He gave His only begotten Son, that whoever believes in Him shall not perish, but have eternal life.* Yes, read the 3rd chapter of Romans if you want to find out how man lost life. Then read the 3rd chapter of John and read it prayerfully and with God's Spirit in you, and you will see how man is to get everlasting life back again. I do not know a chapter that should be read in a more earnest spirit, or read more deeply, than this chapter. It is so plain and reasonable.

If there are a thousand people here tonight who want to know what love God has for them, let them read the 3rd chapter of John, and they will find it there, and find eternal life. They need not go out of this hall tonight to find eternal life. They will find it here in this chapter, and find eternal life before this meeting closes. They hear tonight how the way for salvation of their souls is open to them.

I know nothing more important than this subject of regeneration. I know of nothing in the Bible more important and more plain than this, and yet it is a question that neither the Church nor the world is sound upon. There is no question upon which the Church and the world are more confounded than upon this very question of regeneration. If a man is sound on every other subject, you will probably find that he is unsound on this plain subject of regeneration. Yet it is the very foundation of our hope, and the very foundation of our religion. It is a great deal better, with God's help, to understand this question perfectly first, than to go on further in the Word of God. It is a solemn question – "Am I born of the Spirit? Have I been born again?" For you know that, *unless one is born again he cannot see the kingdom of God*.

Now, let me say what regeneration is not. It is not going to church. Very often I see people and ask them if they are Christians. "Yes, of course I am. At least, I think I am. I go to church every Sunday." Ah, but that is not regeneration. If you go down in the dark alleys and byways of the city, and do all the good you can, preach God's Word, and show God's love to those abandoned beings – I tell you, that is not regeneration. No! It is a false idea that you get regenerated by scattering the seed of God by the wayside. But still there is another class of persons who think they are Christians. They say, "I am trying to do what is right – am I not a Christian? Is not that a new birth?" No; I tell you, no. What has that to do with being born again? There is yet another class – those who have turned over a new leaf and think they are regenerated. But no, forming a new resolution is not being born again. That will not do you any good.

Nor will being baptized do you any good. Yet you hear people say, "Why, I have been baptized, and I was born again when I was baptized." They believe that because they were baptized into the church, they were baptized into the Kingdom of God. I tell you that it is utterly impossible. You may be baptized into the visible church, and yet not be baptized into the Son of God. Baptism is all right in its place. God forbid that I would say anything against it. But if you put that in the place of regeneration, in the place of a new birth, it is a terrible mistake. You cannot be baptized into the Kingdom of God. If I thought I could baptize men into the Kingdom of God, it would be a good deal better for me to do that than to preach. I would get a bucket of water and go up and down the streets, and save men that way. If they would not let me do it while they were awake, I would do it while they were asleep. I would do it anyhow.

Unless one is born again he cannot see the kingdom of God. If anyone here tonight rests his hopes on anything else, – any other foundation, – I pray to God that He may sweep it away from him. You may be baptized into the church, and not be disciples of Jesus Christ. I say to you, do not rest your hopes on that foundation.

Another class says, "I go to the Lord's Supper; I partake uniformly of the Sacrament." Blessed ordinance! Jesus said that as often as we partake, we commemorate His death. Yet, that is not being born again; that is not passing from death unto life. Jesus says plainly, and so plainly that there need not be any mistake about it: *Unless one is born of ... the Spirit he cannot enter into the kingdom of God.* What has a sacrament to do with that? What has going to church to do with being born again? Another man comes up and says, "I say my prayers regularly." Still, I say that that is not being born again. That is not being born of the Spirit.

It is a very solemn question, then, that comes up before us; and oh, that everyone would ask himself earnestly and faithfully: "Have I been born again? Have I been born of the Spirit? Have I passed from death unto life?" There is a class of men who say that these meetings are very good for a certain class of people. That they would be very good if you could get the drunkard here, or get the gambler here, or get other vicious people here – that would do a great deal of good.

There are men, who need to be converted, who might say: "Who did Christ say this to? Who was Nicodemus? Was he a drunkard, a gambler, or a thief?" No! He was one of the very best men in Jerusalem; no doubt about that. He was an honorable councilor; he belonged to the Sanhedrim; he held a very high position; he was one of the best men in the State; he was an orthodox man; he was one of the very soundest men. Why, if he were here today he would be made a President of one of our colleges; he would be put at once at the head of one of our seminaries, and have the "Reverend" put before his name – "Reverend Nicodemus, D.D.," or even "LL.D." And yet what did Christ say to him? *Unless one is born again he cannot see the kingdom of God.* So said He to the woman in the 4th chapter of John.

In the 8th chapter, you see an example of selfrighteousness when the Pharisees were talking to Jesus. Well, there are Pharisees alive today who rely upon their own merits and their own goodness. They say to you, "Oh yes, these meetings are very good for the abandoned, and the outcasts, and the unfortunate; they are very good for immoral men; but we are moral. Tell these things to men who are not moral." They seem to think that when Jesus said, "Ye must be born again," He meant someone else must be born again – that He did not mean them at all. Just imagine some man in Jerusalem seeing John the Beloved walking through the streets, and saying to him, "I met your Master last night. I went round to see Him." John would say, "How did you like Him?" He might reply, "I never met such a person in my life; never heard a man talk as He did. What He told me has been ringing in my ears ever since. He told me that *God so loved the world, that He gave His only begotten Son, that whoever believes in Him shall not perish, but have eternal life.* John, does your Master talk in that way all the time?" "Yes, He always talks in that way." That man will never forget that interview. He was found in the dark by Christ; He was directed into the right way. In that way he will ever continue, and there is not a thing he would not do for Jesus.

See Nicodemus. He, with Joseph of Arimathea, took down the body of Jesus and brought it away, and stood by Jesus to the last. I never knew a man who had a personal interview with Jesus who did not stay by Him. Oh, make up your mind that you will seek Him and follow Him until you have an interview with Him, for no man spoke as that Man spoke. He is just the Man that everyone wants.

But I can imagine someone saying, "If that is having a new birth, what am I to do? I cannot create life. I certainly cannot save myself." You certainly cannot, and we do not preach that you can. We tell you it is utterly impossible to make a man better without Christ, but that is what men are trying to do. They are trying to patch up this "old Adam" nature. There must be a new creation. Regeneration is a new creation, and if it is a new creation, it must be the work of God.

In the 1st chapter of Genesis, man does not appear. There is no one there but God. Man is not there to help or take part. When God created the earth, He was alone. When God redeemed the world, He was alone. *That which is born of the flesh is flesh, and that which is born of the Spirit is spirit* (John 3:6). The Ethiopian cannot change his skin, and the leopard cannot change his spots. When I was in England, my little girl said, "Papa, why don't those colored people wash themselves white?" You might as well try to make yourselves pure and holy without the help of God. It would be just as easy for you to do that as for the black man to wash himself white. The Ethiopian cannot change his skin, neither can the leopard change his spots. A man might just as well try to leap over the moon as to serve God in the flesh. Therefore, *that which is born of the flesh is flesh, and that which is born of the Spirit is spirit.*

Now, God tells us in this chapter how we are to get into His kingdom. We are not to work our way in – not that salvation is not worth working for. We admit all that. If there were rivers and mountains in the way, it would be worth swimming those rivers, and climbing those mountains. There is no doubt that salvation is worth all that, but we do not get it by our works. It is *to the one who does not work, but believes* (Romans 4:5). We work because we are saved; we do not work to be saved. We work from the Cross, not towards it. It is written, *Work out your salvation with fear and trembling* (Philippians 2:12). Why, you must have your salvation before you can work it out. Suppose I say to my little boy, "I want you to spend that hundred dollars carefully." "Well," he says, "let me have the hundred dollars, and I will be careful how I spend it."

I remember when I first left home and went to Boston, I had spent all my money. I went to the post office three times a day. I knew there was only one mail a day from home, but I thought by some possibility there might be a letter for me. At last, I received a letter from my little sister, and oh, glad I was to get it. She had heard that there were a great many pickpockets in Boston, and a large part of that letter was to urge me to be very careful not to let anybody pick my pocket. Now I required to have something in my pocket before I could have it picked. So you must have salvation before you can work it out.

Salvation is *to the one who does not work, but believes.* When Christ cried out on Calvary, "It is finished!" He meant what He said. All that men have to do now is just to accept of the work of Jesus Christ. There is no hope for a man or a woman as long as they are trying to work out salvation for themselves. I can imagine there are some people here who will say, as Nicodemus possibly did, "This is a very mysterious thing." I see the scowl on that Pharisee's brow as he says, "How can these things be?" It sounds very strange to his ear. "Born again; born of the Spirit? How can these things be?" A great many people say, "You must reason it out; but if you do not reason it out, do not ask us to believe it." I can imagine a great many people in this hall saying that. When you ask me to reason it out, I tell you frankly, I cannot do it.

The wind blows where it wishes and you hear the sound of it, but do not know where it comes from and where it is going; so is everyone who is born of the Spirit (John 3:8). I do not understand all about the wind. You ask me to reason it out. I cannot. It may blow due north here, and up at Boston, it may blow due south. I may go up a few hundred feet and find it blowing in an entirely opposite direction from what it is down here. You ask me to explain these currents of wind, but I cannot explain them because I do not understand it. Suppose I stand here and assert, "Oh, there is no such thing as wind." I can imagine that little girl down there saying, "I know more about it than that man does; often have I heard the wind and felt the wind blowing against my face. Did not the wind blow my umbrella out of my hands the other day? Did I not see it blow a man's hat off in the street? Have I not seen it blow the trees in the forests, and the growing corn in the country?"

My friends, you might just as well tell me tonight that there is no wind as tell me there is no such thing as a man being born of the Spirit. I have felt the Spirit of God working in my heart just as really and as truly as I have felt the wind blowing in my face. I cannot reason it out. There are a great many things I cannot reason out, but which I believe. I never could reason out the creation. I can see the world, but I cannot tell how God made it out of nothing. But almost every man will admit there was a creating power. There are a great many things that I cannot explain and that I cannot reason out, and yet that I believe. I heard a commercial traveler say that he had heard that the ministry and religion of Jesus Christ were matters of revelation and not investigation. When God ... was pleased to reveal His Son in me, says Paul (Galatians 1:15-16).

There was a party of young men together, and these young men went into the country. On their journey, they made up their minds not to believe anything they could not reason out. An old man heard them and then said, "I heard you say you would not believe anything you could not reason out." "Yes," they said, "that is so." "Well," he said, "coming down on the train today, I noticed some geese, some sheep, some swine, and some cattle, all eating grass. Can you tell me by what process that same grass was turned into hair, feathers, bristles, and wool? Do you believe it is a fact?" "Oh yes," they said, "we cannot help believing that, though we fail to understand it." "Well," said the old man, "I cannot help believing in Jesus Christ." I cannot help believing in the regeneration of man when I see men that have been reclaimed, when I see men that have been reformed. Have not some of the very worst men in the city been regenerated, picked up out of the pit, and their feet put upon the Rock, and a new song put in their mouths? Their tongues were cursing and blaspheming, and now are occupied in praising God. Old things have passed away and all things have become new. They are not reformed only; they are regenerated – new men in Christ Jesus.

Look you, down there in the dark alleys of New York is a

poor drunkard. I think if you want to get near hell, you should go to a poor drunkard's home. Go to the house of that poor miserable drunkard. Is there anything more like hell on earth? See the want and distress that reign there. But hark! A footstep is heard at the door, and the children run and hide themselves. The patient wife waits to meet the man. He has been her torment. Many a time, she has borne about for weeks the marks of his blows. Many a time, that strong right hand has been brought down on her defenseless head. And now, she waits, expecting to hear his oaths and suffer his brutal treatment. He comes in and says to her: "I have been to the meeting, and I heard there that if I will, I can be converted. I believe that God is able to save me."

Go down to that house again in a few weeks, and what a change! As you approach, you hear someone singing. It is not the song of a reveler, but that good old hymn, "Rock of Ages." The children are no longer afraid of the man but cluster around his knee. His wife is near him, her face lit up with a happy glow. Is not that a picture of regeneration? I can take you to many such homes, made happy by the regenerating power of the religion of Christ. What men want is the power to overcome temptation, the power to lead a right life.

The only way to get into the Kingdom of God is to be born into it. If the Archangel Gabriel were to wing his way here tonight, and we could have a chance to tell him all our wishes, we could not ask him for a better way of getting into the Kingdom of God. Christ made salvation ready for us, and all we have to do is just take it. Oh, may we not hesitate to take it!

There is a law in this land requiring that the president should be born in the country. When foreigners come to our shores, they have no right to complain against such a law, which forbids them from ever becoming Presidents. Now, has not God a right to make a law that all those who become heirs of eternal life must be born into His Kingdom? An unregenerated man would rather be in hell than in heaven. Take a man whose heart is full of corruption and wickedness, and place him in heaven among the pure, the holy, and the redeemed, and he would not want to stay there.

My friends, if we are to be happy in heaven, we must begin to make a heaven here on earth. Heaven is a prepared place for a prepared people. If a gambler or blasphemer were taken out of the streets of New York and placed on the crystal pavement of heaven and under the shadow of the tree of life, he would say, "I do not want to stay here." If men were taken to heaven just as they are by nature, without having their hearts regenerated, there would be another rebellion in heaven. Heaven is filled with a company of those who have been twice born. When I was born in 1837, I received my old Adam nature, and when I was born again in 1856, I had another nature given to me.

It is impossible to serve God properly unless you first make up your mind to be born again. If a house is built upon the sand, it falls; but if it is founded upon a rock, it stands firm against the wind and wave. Our faith can never endure unless it is founded on Christ. We may travel through the earth and see many countries; but there is one country – the land of Beulah, which John Bunyan saw in vision – we will never behold unless we are born again – regenerated by Christ.

We can look abroad and see many beautiful trees, but the tree of life we will never behold unless our eyes are made clear by faith in the Savior. You may see the beautiful rivers of the earth – the Ohio, the Mississippi, the Hudson – and may ride upon their bosoms; but bear in mind that your eye will never rest upon the river which bursts out from the Throne of God and flows through the upper Kingdom, unless you are born again. God has said it, and not man. You will never see the Kingdom of God except you are born again. You may see the kings and lords of the earth, but the King of kings and Lord of lords you will never see except you are born again.

When you are in London you may go to the Tower and see the crown of England, which is worth thousands of pounds, and is guarded there by soldiers; but bear in mind that your eye will never rest upon the crown of life except you are born again. You may come to these meetings and hear the songs of Zion which are sung here; but one song – that of Moses and the Lamb – the uncircumcised ear will never hear: its melody will only gladden the ear of those who have been born again. You may look upon the beautiful mansions of New York and the Hudson, but bear in mind that the mansions which Christ has gone to prepare you will never see unless you are born again. It is God who says it. You may see ten thousand beautiful things in this world, but the city that Abraham caught a glimpse of, and from that time became a pilgrim and sojourner, you will never see unless you are born again (Hebrew 11:8,13,16). Many of you may be invited to marriage feasts here, but you will never attend the marriage supper of the Lamb except you are born again. It is God who says it, dear friends. You may be looking on the face of your sainted mother tonight and feel that she is praying for you; but the time will come when you will never see her more unless you are born again.

I may be speaking to a young man or a young lady who has recently stood by the bedside of a dying mother, and she may have said, "Be sure and meet me in heaven," and you made the promise. Ah! You will never see her again unless you are born again. I believe Jesus of Nazareth sooner than those infidels who say you do not need to be born again. Parents, if you hope to see your children who have gone before, you must be born of the Spirit. I may be speaking tonight to a father and mother who have recently borne a loved one to the grave, and how dark your home seems! Never more will you see your child unless you are born again. If you wish to be reunited to your loved ones you must be born again. I may be speaking to a father and mother who have a loved one up yonder, and if you could hear that loved one's voice, it would say, "Come this way." Have not some of you a sainted friend up yonder? Young man or young lady, have you not a mother in the world of light? If you could hear her speak, would not she say, "Come this way, my son," – "Come this way, my daughter"? If you would ever see her again, you must be born again.

We all have an Elder Brother there. Nearly nineteen hundred years ago, He crossed over, and from the heavenly shores, He is calling you to heaven. Let us turn our backs upon the world. Let us give a deaf ear to the world. Let us get our heart in the Kingdom of God and cry, "Life! Life! Eternal life!"

Let us pray that God may keep every soul now here from going out of this building tonight without being born again!

CHAPTER 9

THE SON OF MAN LIFTED UP

As Moses lifted up the serpent in the wilderness, even so must the Son of Man be lifted up.
– John 3:14

Those who heard my last address will remember that I was speaking upon the text in the 3rd chapter of John: *You must be born again.* I want to call your attention tonight to the little word "must," in the same chapter. *Even so "must" the Son of Man be lifted up* (John 3:14). I now come to the remedy, for, when it was time to close my address, I had not had an opportunity of taking up that part of the subject. I want, on this occasion, to take up the matter where I left off. Possibly some went away disappointed after hearing the statement that they must be born again. They may have said, "I do wish he had not left off so soon; I wish he had gone on and told me how I can be born again." God helping me, I will try to tell you this tonight; and I would ask, while I try to do so, that Christians would lift up their hearts in prayer to God, that the way be made so plain that a great number may come into the kingdom of God.

Let us see how God is able to save unto the uttermost. I want you to read the 14th and 15th verses of this chapter: *As Moses lifted up the serpent in the wilderness, even so must the Son of Man be lifted up; so that whoever believes will in Him have eternal life. That* whoever *believes will in Him have eternal life.* Mark that! Let me tell you who are unsaved within these walls tonight what God has done for you. He has done everything that He could do toward your salvation. You need not wait for God to do anything more. In one place, He asks the question, what more could He have done (Isaiah 5:4). He sent His prophets, and they killed them, and then He sent His beloved Son, and they murdered Him. And now, He has sent the Holy Spirit to convince us of sin and to show how we are to be saved. We are all sinners, and every man and woman know in their hearts that they are sinners.

Now, we come here tonight to point out the remedy for sin, and to tell you how you are to be saved from sin. Jesus came into the world to seek and to save that which was lost (Luke 19:10), and you know there is no other name under heaven that has been given among men by which we must be saved, but the name of Jesus Christ our Lord (Acts 4:12). And again, You shall call His name Jesus, for He will save His people from their sins (Matthew 1:21). No sinner need die if he but put his trust in Christ. There is no salvation in anything else, nor in any other name. The apostles preached no other doctrine, nor any other name. All their testimony was that Christ died for our sakes.

Take the 2nd chapter of Acts, and you may read from there on through all the chapters, and there is hardly one but speaks of Christ's death and of Christ crucified; of Christ dying for you; rising again for you; ascending into Heaven for you; and coming again for you. That is the gospel of St. Paul and of St. Peter. That is the gospel that Stephen preached when they stoned him to death. Paul preached that gospel at Antioch, Corinth, and Ephesus. Yes, Christ crucified – that is the remedy for sin.

We hear a great many men murmur because God permitted

sin to come into the world. They say it is a great mystery. Well, I say too, it is a great mystery. A Christian minister and writer has well said, that although it was a great mystery how sin came into the world, it was a greater mystery how God came to bear the brunt of it Himself. We might talk all the time about the origin of sin; how it came into the world, but that would in no way help you. If I see a man tumble into the river, and about to drown, it will do no good for me to sit down and bow my head and indulge in deep thought and reasoning as to how he came to get in there. The great question would then be – how to get him out of there. Just look over your own life. You can prove that you are a sinner and have need of repentance; or if you cannot do it to your own satisfaction, there are some of your neighbors, no doubt, who can do it for you.

And right here comes in the remedy for sin. In the 3rd chapter of John, we are told how men are to be saved, namely, by Him who was lifted up on the cross. Just as Moses lifted up the brazen serpent in the wilderness, so must the Son of Man be lifted up, *whoever believes in Him shall not perish, but have eternal life.* And here some men complain and say that it is very unreasonable that they would be held responsible for the sin of a man six thousand years ago. It was not long ago that a man was talking to me about the injustice of being condemned on account of a man having sinned six thousand years ago.

If there is a man here tonight who is going to answer in that way, I tell him it will not do him any good. If you are lost, it will not be on account of Adam's sin. "Well," some will say, "that is a strange statement for you to make, Mr. Moody." Well, I dare say you do think it strange. I wonder what some of the theologians who are present here tonight think of it. What do some of the ministers on this platform say to it? I would like to know. Yet, let me say it again, it will not be on account of Adam's sin that you will be lost, if you are lost. "Why, Mr. Moody, that is a paradox. How do you explain that?"

Well, let me illustrate it then, and perhaps you will be able to understand it. Suppose I am dying of consumption, which I inherited from my father or mother. I did not get it by any fault of my own, by any neglect of my health; I inherited it, let us suppose. Well, I go to the best physicians, and they all give me up. They say that I am incurable; that I must die; and at length, that I have only thirty days to live. Well, a friend happens to come along and looks at me and says: "Moody, you are in consumption." I reply, "I know it very well. I don't want anyone to tell me that." "But," he says, there is a remedy – a remedy, I tell you. Let me have your attention; I want to call your attention to this. I tell you there is a remedy." "But, sir, I don't believe it. I have tried the leading physicians in this country and in Europe, and they tell me there is no hope." "But you know me, Moody; you have known me for years." "Yes, sir." "Do you think, then, I would tell you a falsehood?" "No." "Well, ten years ago I was as far gone. I was given up by the physicians to die, but I took this medicine, and it cured me. I am perfectly well. Look at me." I say that it is "a very strange case." "Yes, it may be strange, but it is a fact. This medicine cured me; take this medicine and it will cure you. Although it has cost me a great deal, it will not cost you anything. Do not make light of it, I beg of you." "Well," I say, "I would like to believe you, but this is contrary to my reason."

Hearing this, my friend goes away and returns with another friend, and he testifies to the same thing. He again goes away when I do not yet believe, and brings in another friend, and another, and another, and another, and they all testify to the same thing. They say they were as bad as myself; that they took the same medicine that has been offered to me; and that it cured them. He then hands me the medicine. I dash it to the ground. I do not believe in its saving power; I die. The reason is then that I spurned the remedy. So, if you perish, it will not be because Adam fell, but because you spurn the remedy offered to you to save you. You will choose darkness rather than light. How then will you escape, if you neglect so great salvation? There is no hope for you if you neglect the remedy. It does no good to look at the wound. If we had been in the Israelitish camp and had been bitten by one of the fiery serpents, it would have done no good to look at the wound. Looking at a wound will never save anyone. What you must do is to look at the remedy, to look away to Him who has power to save you from your sin.

Behold the camp of the Israelites; look at the scene that is pictured to your eyes. And now look at New York City today. There, in that past age, and right here in the present age, all – all are dying because they neglect the remedy that is offered.

In that arid desert is many a short and tiny grave; many a child has been bitten by the fiery serpents. Fathers and mothers are bearing away their children. Over yonder they are just burying a mother; a loved mother is about to be laid in the earth. All the family, weeping, gather around the beloved form. You hear the mournful cries; you see the bitter tears. The father is being borne away to his last resting place. There is wailing going up all over the camp. Tears are pouring down for thousands who have passed away; thousands more are dying, and the plague is raging from one end of the camp to the other.

I see in one tent an Israelitish mother bending over the form of a beloved boy, just coming into the bloom of life, just budding into manhood. She is wiping away the sweat of death that is gathering upon his brow. Yet a little while, and his eyes are fixed and glassy, for life is ebbing fast away. The mother's heartstrings are torn and bleeding. All at once she hears a shout in the camp. A great shout goes up. What does it mean? She goes to the door of the tent. "What is this noise in the camp?"

she asks those passing by, and someone says: "Why, my good woman, haven't you heard the good news that has come into the camp?" "No," says the woman, "Good news! What is it?" "Why, haven't you heard about it? God has provided a remedy." "What! for the bitten Israelites? Oh, tell me what the remedy is!"

"God has instructed Moses to make a brazen serpent and put it on a pole in the middle of the camp. He has declared that whosoever looks upon it shall live. The shout that you hear is the shout of the people when they see the serpent lifted up." The mother goes back into the tent, and she says: "My boy, I have good news to tell you. You need not die. My boy, my boy, I have come with good tidings; you can live." He is already getting stupefied; he is so weak he cannot walk to the door of the tent. She puts her strong arms under him and lifts him up. "Look yonder; look right there under the hill." But the boy does not see anything; he says, "I don't see anything. What is it, mother?" And she says: "Keep looking, and you will see it." At last, he catches a glimpse of the glistening serpent, and he is well. And thus, it is with many a young convert. Some men say, "Oh, we don't believe in sudden conversions." How long did it take to cure that boy? How long did it take to cure those serpentbitten Israelites? It was just a look, and they were well.

That Hebrew boy is a young convert. I can fancy that I see him now calling on all those who were with him to praise God. He sees another young man bitten as he was, and he runs up to him and tells him, "You need not die." "Oh," the young man replies, "I cannot live; it is not possible. There is not a physician in Israel who can cure me." He does not know he has not to die. "Why, have you not heard the news? God has provided a remedy." "What remedy?" "Why, God has told Moses to lift up a brazen serpent and has said that none of those who look upon that serpent will die."

I can just imagine the young man. He may be what you

call an intellectual young man. He says to the young convert: "You don't think I am going to believe anything like that? If the physicians in Israel cannot cure me, you don't think than an old brass serpent on a pole is going to cure me?" "Why, sir, I was as bad as yourself!" "You don't say so!" "Yes, I do." "That is the most astonishing thing I ever heard," says the young man. "I wish you would explain the philosophy of it." "I cannot, I only know that I looked at that serpent, and I was cured. That did it. I just looked; that is all. My mother told me the reports that were being heard through the camp, and I just believed what my mother said, and I am perfectly well." "Well, I don't believe you were bitten as badly as I have been." The young man pulls up his sleeve. "Look there! That mark shows where I was bitten, and I tell you I was worse than you are." "Well, if I understood the philosophy of it, I would look and get well." "Let go of your philosophy; *look and live.*" "But, sir, you ask me to do an unreasonable thing. If God had said, 'Take the brass and rub it into the wound, there might be something in the brass that would cure the bite.' Young man, explain the philosophy of it." I see some people before me who have talked in that way since I have been here. But the young man calls in another and takes him into the tent and says: "Just tell him how the Lord saved you," and he tells just the same story. He calls in others, and they all say the same thing.

And so it is with the religion of Jesus Christ. One and another tells the same story; and by and by, all God's people will tell how they have been all saved in one way – by Jesus of Nazareth. No other name, no other way. If all nations could talk one language, they would only tell one story, *one name,* one remedy.

The young man says it is a very strange thing. "If the Lord had told Moses to go and get some herbs, or some plants and roots, and stew them and take the medicine, there would be something in that. But it is so contrary to my nature to do such a thing as look at the serpent, that I cannot do it." "You can do it." At length, his mother, who has been out in the camp comes in, and she says, "My boy, I have just the best news in the world for you. I was in the camp, and I saw hundreds who were very far gone, and they are all perfectly well now." The young man says: "I would like to get well; it is a very painful thought to die. I want to go into the promised land, and it is terrible to die here in this wilderness. But the fact is, I don't understand the remedy. It does not appeal to my reason. I can't believe that I can get well in a moment." And the young man dies in consequence of his own unbelief.

Whose fault is it – the unbelief here? Whose fault is it? God provided a remedy for this bitten Israelite – "Look and live!" And there is eternal life for every poor bitten Israelite here. Look, and you can be saved, my friends. This very night God has provided a remedy, and it is offered to all. The trouble is, a great many people are looking at the pole. Do not look at the pole; that does no good. That is the church. You need not look at the church; the church is all right, but the church cannot save you. Look beyond the pole. Look at the Crucified One. Look at Calvary. Bear in mind, sinner, that Jesus died for all. Look in time, and *you* will be saved if there is no one else. If Christ opened the way, it is the way. What other name is there given whereby we can be saved? We do not want to look at Moses; Moses is all right in his place, but Moses cannot save you. You need not look at these ministers; they are just God's chosen instruments to hold up the remedy, to hold up Christ. And so, my friends, take your eyes off of men, take your eyes off of the church. But lift them up to Jesus, who took away the sin of the world, and there will be life from this hour.

Thank God, we do not require an education to teach us how to look. That little girl who cannot read, that little boy, four years old, who cannot read, can look. When the father is coming home, the mother says to her little boy, "Look! look! look!" and the little child learns to look long before he is a year old. And that is the way to be saved. It is to look at the Lamb of God that takes away the sin of the world; and there is life tonight and this moment for every man who is willing to look. Not to look at the Church, not to look at yourselves, but to look at Christ. Some people say, "There is a man; what faith he has, I wish I had his faith." You might as well say, "I wish I had his eyes." You do not need his faith; what you need is his Christ. You need not be wishing for his eyes. You have eyes of your own.

Some men say, "I wish I knew how to be saved." Just take God at His word and trust His Son this very night, this very hour, this very moment. He will save you if you trust Him. I imagine I hear someone saying, "I don't feel the bite as much as I wish I could. I know I'm a sinner and all that, but I don't feel the bite enough." How much do you want to feel it? How much does God want you to feel it? When I was in Belfast, I knew a doctor who had a friend, a leading surgeon there, and he told me that the surgeon's custom was, before performing any operation, to say to the patient, "Take a good look at the wound, and then fix your eyes on me, and don't take them off till I get through." I thought at the time that was a good illustration.

Sinner, take a good look at the wound tonight, and then fix your eyes on Christ, and do not take them off. It is better to look at the remedy than at the wound. See what a poor wretched sinner you are, and then look at the Lamb of God that takes away the sin of the world. He died for the ungodly and the sinner. Say "I'll take Him," and may God help you to lift your eye to the Man on Calvary. And as the Israelites looked upon the serpent and were healed, so may you look and live tonight.

After the battle of Pittsburgh Landing and Murfreesboro, I was in a hospital at Murfreesboro. In the middle of the night, I was aroused and told that a man in one of the wards wanted to see me. I went to him, and he called me "chaplain" – I was not a chaplain – and said he wanted me to help him to die. And I said, "I'd take you right up in my arms and carry you into the kingdom of God if I could; but I can't do it. I can't help you to die!" And he said, "Who can?" I said, "The Lord Jesus Christ can. He came for that purpose." He shook his head, and said, "He can't save me; I have sinned all my life." And I said, "But He came to save sinners."

I thought of his mother in the North, and I was sure that she was anxious that he would die right, and I resolved I would stay with him. I prayed two or three times, and repeated all the promises I could, for it was evident that, in a few hours, he would be gone. I said I wanted to read him a conversation that Christ had with a man who was anxious about his soul. I turned to the 3rd chapter of John. His eyes were riveted on me, and when I came to the 14th and 15th verses – my text tonight – he caught up the words, "As Moses lifted up the serpent in the wilderness, even so must the Son of Man be lifted up; so that whoever believes will in Him have eternal life." He stopped me and said, "Is that there?" I said "Yes." He asked me to read it again, and I did so.

He leaned his elbows on the cot and clasped his hands together and said, "That's good; won't you read it again?" I read it the third time and then went on with the rest of the chapter. When I finished, his eyes were closed, his hands were folded, and there was a smile on his face. Oh, how it was lit up! What a change had come over it! I saw his lips quivering, and I leaned over him and heard, in a faint whisper, *As Moses lifted up the serpent in the wilderness, even so must the Son of Man be lifted up; so that whoever believes will in Him have eternal life.* He opened his eyes and said, "That's enough; don't read any more." He lingered a few hours, pillowing his head on those two verses, and then went up in one of Christ's chariots, and took his seat in the Kingdom of God.

You may spurn God's remedy and perish; but I tell you, God does not want you to perish. *As I live! declares the Lord God, I take no pleasure in the death of the wicked, but rather that the wicked turn from his way and live. Turn back, turn back from your evil ways! Why then will you die?* (Ezekiel 33:11). May God help you all to look unto the Lord Jesus Christ and be saved.

CHAPTER 10

THE LOVE OF CHRIST

The love of Christ which surpasses knowledge.
– Ephesians 3:19

I want to take for our subject tonight what Christ is to us, and when I am done, if any one here present says he is not convinced, it will be because he does not want to be convinced and will not have Christ. He will be all that I make Him out to be, and a thousand times more. No man living could tell in an hour about His great love and His great worth; no, he could not tell it in twentyfour hours. It is beyond time and expression to tell what Christ is to us, that is, if we have believed on Him and been redeemed by Him. I remember speaking upon this subject some time ago in Europe, and when I had concluded my address and was going home, I said to a Scotch friend who accompanied me, that I was very much disappointed; that I did not get through with the subject. He looked at me in astonishment and said, "My friend, what! Did you expect to tell what Christ is in half an hour? You need never expect to finish telling it through all eternity; you would never get through with it." I have thought of it often since. Take eternity! Yes, I know it would.

Well, right here I want to ask you whether Christ is worth having? I imagine some of you will say that this is a strange question – that it is strange for a man to get up and ask this. Well, perhaps it is, but it does seem to me that a great many men do think that Christ is not worth having. If they do really want Him, let them take Him. He was God's greatest gift to the world. He is there for you and for me to accept. Just let me ask that question again: Do you think that the Son of God is worth having? Oh, that God may open the eyes of every soul here tonight to behold Christ right in the midst! Oh, that you may worship Him in spirit and in truth, view Him as the chiefest among ten thousand, the One altogether lovely! Christ wants to be a Savior to every one of us.

In the second chapter of Luke and the tenth and eleventh verses, we read that a Savior has been given us: *Behold, I bring you good news of great joy which will be for all the people; for today in the city of David there has been born for you a Savior, who is Christ the Lord.* And if we would know Him as our Lord, and truth, and wisdom, and life, we must first know Him as our Savior. You must first meet Him at Calvary, first see Him on the cross. There is no life in us except we come to Calvary. Mind, I do not ask you to trust in the mere form of godliness. Many, yes thousands, make that great mistake. They are not taking Christ as their personal Savior; they do not know Him as their own. That is a great mistake, and it is a common mistake.

During the last few years, I have not been occupied so much with the person of Christ; it has been more about the doctrine and the form. But recently, Christ has become more to me personally. And it would be a great help to you to cultivate His acquaintance personally, come to Him as a personal Savior, and be able to take Him and look up to Him and say, "He is my Savior." I do not know how many times I have heard men say during the past few weeks, "I would come to Him and love

Him, but I don't think I could hold out." But I tell you, He is not only a Savior, but a Deliverer. He can deliver us from the power of sin. He can deliver us from Satan. There is not a guilt, crime, trouble, or trial, from which the Son of God is not able to deliver us if we go to Him.

Bear in mind that we are the lawful captives of sin. If a man has committed a sin, Satan has a power over him and a claim upon him, and holds him as his lawful prey. But said the Lord, Even the captives of the mighty man will be taken away (Isaiah 49:25). And He said further in Isaiah 49:24-26 that He will contend for you and take you from those that hold you captive. Thanks be to God, we can go to Him with confidence, and have Him deliver us from the power of our besetting sin. If there is a man here who is the slave of strong drink, I bring him good news! God is able to deliver you from that which has gained the mastery over you. If there is a man here who is the slave of any passion or any lust, I say unto him that the Son of God came into the world to destroy the works of the devil and deliver you from the power of Satan; He wants to deliver not only you, but to deliver every soul. And you can, if you will, be saved this very minute.

When He led the children of Israel out from Egypt and through the Red Sea, He saved them at once. So can everyone be saved, no matter what church he belongs to, whether he belongs to the true Apostolic church, or to any other church. The Son of God can save in any church or in any denomination. You can be saved in any church if you follow Him. He says, *I am the way, and the truth, and the life* (John 14:6). The Son of God will be in the right church; He makes no mistake. He never leads His people into a wrong path. Christ is the way. He said unto Peter, "Follow Me," and Peter followed Him and found everlasting life. Who can lead people through the wilderness but the Lord Almighty? He created the wilderness, and He knows it better than anyone else. He will take care that none of His children are lost. He will put before them the pillar of fire, and the pillar of cloud.

No man that follows in the footsteps of Christ can be in the wrong way. Christ says, I am the way. Yes, but some people say, "That is the old way. I want something new." But I say unto you that the old way is the best and the only way. The way, young man, that your sainted mother walked is the right way. Do not go any other way. When men who do not believe in Christ come and say they have found a new way, do not believe them. Do not believe these infidels. They want to take the Bible from you. But what do they intend to give you in its place? They call to you to give up your Bible, but what can they do for you without that? They might offer you Paine's "Age of Reason"! What a book to put in the place of our beloved Bible! Why, even the infidels will not have it themselves. What consolation, what comfort, what joy could be obtained from such a book as they would give to you? What pain would it assuage? What comfort would it bring to you? They say, "We have grown wiser than the Bible now; it is an old wornout Book."

Why, on the same principle they might complain of the sun; and yet what would they put in the place of its warmth, its genial influence, its lifegiving power? Let them give up the sun then, and try to supply the world with gaslight. The sun is thousands of years old, but gas is new: use gas then in place of the sun. Block up all the windows of your houses, and have nothing to do with the sun. You might as well do that as give up the Bible. Outgrown it! Why, there is no book to be compared with it. No other book will lift up the world. Try and bring up your children without the Bible, and see what they will come to. If you could go into a town where men were trying to live without that good book, you would flee from it as they who left Sodom and Gomorrah. Have the infidels ever produced a Knox, a Bunyan, or a Milton?

When a man goes into the wilderness to hunt, he takes a hatchet with him and cuts the bark off the trees – they call it "blazing" – and thus he can find his way out; or others can follow in his track. So, Christ has blazed the way along. He has gone up on high, and He says, "Follow Me." Just come now and follow the Son of God, for there is life there.

But there is more even than this. He is the Light upon our way. Now, I hear so many people complaining about the darkness, but there is no darkness in following Christ. I have seen a picture that I do not very much care about. It represents Christ knocking at the door with a lantern. What does the Son of God want with a lantern? Christ says, *I am the Light of the world* (John 8:12). He needs no lantern. Did you ever know a man or woman anywhere in Christendom who was following the Son of God and yet was in darkness? You never did. Not only that, you never will. A man who is following Christ cannot but be in the light, because Christ is the Light of the world. Yes, and He lightens us beyond the grave and beyond the Judgment. We fear not death. The valley of the shadow of death cannot be very dark, because Christ is there, and He will be in the way. Have you not stood at the bedside of a dying saint? Have you not seen the light that streamed in there, and thought you were just at the very portals of Heaven? Do you know why it was light there? Why, the curtain was lifted, and, like Stephen, the dying one could look into the Celestial City?

A great many people are seeking for peace and are seeking for joy, and they hear this minister and that minister, and this person and that person, speak about peace and joy. You just follow Christ, and peace will come of itself. When I was a little boy, I used to try to catch my shadow, but I always failed. Many times, I tried to jump over the shadow of my head; many times,

I tried to see if I could not outrun my shadow, but it always kept ahead of me. But I turned round and faced the sun; lo and behold, my shadow was coming after me. And so we want to look toward Christ, and peace and joy and happiness will come in turn. We do not want to turn our backs to the light, but to keep our eyes upon Christ.

Look unto Jesus, the author and finisher of our faith; do not look to see what neighbor Jones is doing, to see if we are not better than he is. We will never get peace in that way. What is the standard? *Look up.* Look up tonight, because there is darkness around us. We are not to look around us, but we are to keep looking up. Christ is the Light of the world, and you know the world refused to have the light; they put it out. They took Him to Calvary, and they put Him to death. Just before they put that Light out, He said to His disciples, "You are the light of the world." What Christ has left us down here for – is to shine. We are not put here to make money, but that we may shine like Daniel in Babylon; and if man will let his light shine – the Bible does not say, make it shine – the light will shine out of our countenance, and the world will see there is a living reality in the religion of Jesus Christ.

In the darkest hours in the history of our country, when it looked as if everything was going to pieces, I remember attending a prayermeeting one Sunday night. Every speaker spoke of the dark ride. But an old man, the light shining out of his eyes, and his beautiful white hair falling over his shoulders, said, "You do not talk like true sons of the King. Up around the throne, it is all light. If an unconverted man were to come in here and listen to you, he certainly would not wish to become a Christian."

He said he had just come from the East, and he had heard one of his friends talk about a beautiful sunrise. He made arrangements with the landlord to take him up on the summit to see the sunrise. So, in the morning, the guide aroused him, and they started out. The guide went ahead and he followed. They had not journeyed long when a terrible thunderstorm came upon them. The old man said to the guide, "It will be no use to go up. We cannot see the sun rise; the storm is fearful." "Oh, sir," said the guide, "I think we will get above the storm." They could see the lightning playing about them, and the great old mountain shook with the thunder, and it was very dark. But when they passed up above the clouds, all was light and clear. So if it is dark here, rise higher; it is light enough up around the throne. If I may rise up to the light, I have no business to be in darkness. Rise higher, higher, higher. It is the privilege of the child of God to walk on unclouded ground.

Sinner, look up from this night and this hour. Now I do not know but that there may be some infidel, some skeptic here. I heard of an infidel once who said, "Look at your convert; it is all moonshine." The young convert replied to him, "I thank you for the compliment. We are perfectly willing to be called that. The moon borrows the light from the sun, and so we borrow ours from Christ." And so bear in your minds, my friends, that we borrow our light from Christ.

In the 121st Psalm, it is written, Behold, He who keeps Israel will neither slumber nor sleep. The Lord is your keeper. If He is our keeper, can anything hurt us? Keep this in your hearts: Christ is able to save you. He is not only able to light you upon the way, but He is able to keep you from this night and from this hour, until He presents you before the throne without spot and without blemish (Jude 24). Do not tell me He does not have the power to keep you. He has. One object for which Christ came into the world was to keep sinners (2 Timothy 1:12).

Some men have an idea that when they get converted, they have to keep Christ and themselves too. They are all wrong. I remember one time, my little girl was teasing her mother to get her a muff. So, one day, her mother brought a muff home, and, although it was stormy, she very naturally wanted to go out in order to try her new muff. She tried to get me to go out with her. I went out with her, and I said, "Emma, better let me take your hand." She wanted to keep her hands in her muff, and so she refused to take my hand. Well, by and by, she came to an icy place; her little feet slipped, and down she went. When I helped her up, she said, "Papa, you may give me your little finger." "No, my daughter, just take my hand." "No, no, papa, give me your little finger." Well, I gave my finger to her, and for a little way she got along nicely; but soon we came to another icy place, and again she fell. This time she hurt herself a little, and she said, "Papa, give me your hand." So I gave her my hand, closed my fingers about her wrist, and held her up so that she could not fall.

Just so is God our keeper. He is wiser than we. Run to your Elder Brother for aid. Is there a man here to whom a saloon is a temptation – who cannot go by a saloon without wanting to go in? Just let him throw himself upon the Lord. Say, "Lord Jesus, keep me."

There are thousands and millions around the throne of God tonight, who were kept by the power of God. Yes, God gave them grace, and overcame all things for them. Thank God, oh thank God, for that!

When I was in England, I had a great curiosity to visit some zoological gardens because of a story I had heard concerning them. There was a man who had a little dog which he had trained to run. One day, he made a bet about his dog's running, but when the time came for the race, the little dog would not run at all, and the man lost his money. This so enraged the man that he beat the dog terribly, and at last, he thrust him into the lion's cage. He thought the lion would make quick work of him, but the lion lapped the dog and made a pet of him.

At last, the man wanted to get his dog back, and he called

to him and tried by every means to make the little dog come out of the cage, but he would not come. So, the man went and told the keeper. When the keeper came, the man said to him, "That's my dog in the cage there, and I want you to get him out for me." Then the keeper said, "How came the dog there?" The man had to tell him, and the keeper said, "If you want your dog, you can take him out of the cage." He could not take him out, and there he stayed. The only safety for us is to keep close to Christ. The Lion of the tribe of Judah conquered the lion of hell. Keep close to Christ. No one will pluck you out of His hand. It is no delusion He has kept me for twenty years.

The Lord is my shepherd, I shall not want. Ah, what a shepherd! The shepherd takes care of the sheep. Did you ever hear of the sheep taking care of the shepherd? Strive to get into the fold. *The Lord is my shepherd.* Oh, what a good shepherd.

But I want to speak of another thing that the Lord is. He is a burden bearer. I will not speak of His wisdom, righteousness, strength, power; it would take all eternity to tell all about Christ. But I will speak of Him as a bearer of burdens. There is not a poor, sinweary mortal that may not at once cast his burden upon Christ. Cast all your burden upon the Lord. People sometimes pray to have their burden taken from them; and then they will rise up and take their burdens on their shoulders and go away unrelieved. I like to think of Christ as the burden bearer. A minister was moving his library upstairs. His little boy wanted to help him, so he gave him the biggest book he could find, and the little fellow tugged at it till he got it about halfway up. Then, he sat down and cried. His father found him and just took him in his arms, big book and all, and carried him upstairs. So Christ will carry you and all your burdens.

CHAPTER II

GRACE

Full of grace and truth. – John 1:14

I am here going to take a subject rather than a text. I want to talk to you about *free grace*. I say, "free grace." Perhaps I had better drop the word "free," and just say "grace." There is a sermon in the very meaning of the word. It is one of those words that are very little understood at the present time, like the word "gospel." There are a great many who are partakers of the Spirit of Christ, or of grace, who do not know the meaning of the word. I think it is a good plan to go to Webster's Dictionary and look up the meaning of these words that we hear so often, but do not fully understand. You seldom go into a religious assembly, but you hear the word "grace." Yet I was a partaker of the grace of God for years before I knew what it meant. I could not tell the difference between grace and law.

Grace means unlimited mercy, undeserved favor, or unmerited love. I had a man come to see me, and his plea was that he was not fit to be saved. He said there was no hope for him because he had sinned all his life, and there was nothing good in him. I was very much gratified to hear him say that. There is hope for that man, and there is hope for any man who thinks there is nothing good in him. That was the lesson Christ tried to teach the Jews – the lesson of grace. But they were trying to prove themselves to be better than other people. They were of the seed of Abraham and under the Mosaic law, and they thought themselves better than the people about them.

Now let us get at the source of this stream, which has been flowing through the world these hundreds of years. You know that men have been trying to find the source of the Nile. Would it not be as profitable to try and find the source of grace, since this is a stream in which we are all interested? I want to call your attention to the 1st chapter of John, the 14th verse: *And the Word became flesh, and dwelt among us and we saw His glory, glory as of the only begotten from the Father, full of grace and truth.* Then the 17th verse: *For the Law was given through Moses; grace and truth were realized through Jesus Christ.* Then in the 5th chapter of Romans, the 15th verse: *But the free gift is not like the transgression. For if by the transgression of the one the many died, much more did the grace of God and the gift by the grace of the one Man, Jesus Christ, abound to the many.* There it is called the free gift – it abounded unto many.

Then in Paul's first epistle to the Corinthians, the 1st chapter, and the 3rd and 4th verses: Grace to you and peace from God our Father and the Lord Jesus Christ. I thank my God always concerning you for the grace of God which was given you in Christ Jesus. Now bear in mind that He is the God of all grace (1 Peter 5:10). We would know nothing about grace if it were not for Jesus Christ. Men talk about grace, but they do not know much about it. These bankers, they talk about grace. If you want to borrow a thousand dollars and can give good security, they will let you have it and take your note. You give your note and say, "So many months after date, I promise to pay a thousand dollars." Then they give you what they call three days' grace, but they make you pay interest for those three days. That is not grace.

Then, when your note comes due, if you can only pay nine hundred and fifty dollars, they would sell everything you have and make you pay the remaining fifty dollars. Grace consists in giving the principal, interest, and all. I tell you, if you want to get any grace, you must know God. He is *the God of all grace* (1 Peter 5:10). He wants to deal in grace; He wants to deal out unmerited mercy, undeserved favor, unmerited love. If God had not loved man until he was worthy of His love, He would not have loved him at all; for, of himself, man would never have been worthy. God is the God of all grace.

Unto whom does He offer grace? I would like you to turn to three or four texts in your Bibles: to the 21st chapter of Matthew, from the 28th to the 31st verses: *But what do you think? A man had two sons, and he came to the first and said, "Son, go work today in the vineyard." And he answered, "I will not"; but afterward he regretted it and went. The man came to the second and said the same thing; and he answered, "I will, sir"; but he did not go. Which of the two did the will of his father? They said, "The first." Jesus said to them, "Truly I say to you that the tax collectors and prostitutes will get into the kingdom of God before you."* Why? Was it because He loved those publicans and harlots more than He did those Pharisees? No. It was because they would not repent, would not accept grace. They did not believe they needed the grace of God.

A man who believes that he is lost is near salvation. Why? Because you have not to labor to convince him that he is lost. Here is a man who said he would not go and work in his father's vineyard. Afterward, he saw that he had been wrong and repented and went; and this man was the man that grace held up. God will save any man or woman here tonight who will repent and turn to Him. What your life has been in the past makes no difference. He will turn to any who will turn to Him.

I was preaching one Sunday in a church where there was a fashionable audience, and after I had finished the sermon, I said: "If there are any who would like to tarry a little while, and speak to me, I will be glad to talk with them." They all rose up, turned around, and went out. I felt as though I was abandoned. When I was going out, I saw a man standing behind the stove. He was in shabby clothes and was weeping bitterly. I said, "My friend, what is your trouble?" He replied, "You told me tonight that I could be saved; that the grace of God would reach me. You told me that there was not a man so far gone but that the grace of God would reach him." He added: "I am an exile from my family; I have wasted twenty thousand dollars through drink. I have drunk up the coat off my back. But if there is hope for a poor sinner like me, I would like to be saved." It was just like a refreshing glass of water to talk to that man. I dared not give him money, for fear that he would drink it up, but I found him a place at which to stay that night, took an interest in him, and provided him some clothes. Six months later, when I left Chicago for Europe, that man was an earnest Christian. The Lord had blessed him wonderfully. He was an active, capable man.

The grace of God can save just such if they will only repent. I do not care how low a man has fallen; the grace of God can purge him of all sin and place him among the blessed. In proportion as man is a sinner, so much the more does the grace of God abound. There is not a man living to whom the grace of God will not give the victory, if he will only accept it.

I want you to turn for a moment to a passage you will find in the 7th chapter of Mark, verses 24 through 29: *Jesus got up and went away from there to the region of Tyre. And when He had entered a house, He wanted no one to know of it; yet He could not escape notice. But after hearing of Him, a woman whose little daughter had an unclean spirit immediately came and fell at His feet. Now the woman was a Gentile, of the Syrophoenician race. And she kept asking Him to cast the demon out of her daughter. And He was saying to her, "Let the children be satisfied first, for it is not good to take the children's bread and throw it to the dogs." But she answered and said to Him, "Yes, Lord, but even the dogs under the table feed on the children's crumbs." And He said to her, "Because of this answer go; the demon has gone out of your daughter."* Now, just see how Christ dealt with that woman – a Syrian, a Gentile; she did not belong to the seed of Abraham at all. He came to save His own, but His own received Him not. Christ was willing to show grace to the Jews. He dealt in grace with a liberal hand, but those He was desirous to shower grace upon would not take it.

But this woman belonged to a different people. Just read her story. I wonder what would happen if Christ would come and speak in that way now. Suppose He would come into this assembly and call any woman here a dog. Why, that Syrian woman might have said, "Call me a dog! Talk to me like that! Why, I know a woman belonging to the seed of Abraham who lives down near me, and she is the worst and wickedest woman in the neighborhood. I am as good as she is any day." She might have gone away without a blessing, if she had not felt her utter destitution and her lost condition. But Jesus spoke of her as a dog, just to try her. She gave no angry retort, but only broke forth into a despairing cry, "Yes, Lord; yes, Lord." Christ had said it was more blessed to give than to receive. She took the low place and received His blessing. She was satisfied to be given only a crumb, as long as He heard her petition. So, instead of giving her a crumb, He bestowed a whole loaf. And so will you get the fullest beneficence of Christ if you lift your up heart to Him. Oh, that many would but just take this woman's place, understand how low and unworthy they are, and cry unto Jesus! If you do, Christ will lift you up and bless you.

But then the great trouble is that people will not confess that they have need of grace. Such miserable Pharisaism is the worst feature of the present time. They think they can get salvation without the grace of God. The old saying is that when you come to Jesus as a beggar, you go away as a prince. Instead of doing that, they feel so selfconfident and proud that they come always as princes and go away beggars. If you want the Son of God to deal with you, come as a beggar, and He will have mercy upon you. Look at the great crowd going up to the Temple; they feel they have strength of themselves, and all pass on, proud and haughty, except one poor man, who smites himself on the breast and says, "God be merciful to me, a sinner!"

If you want to see the idea that the Jews had as to who was worthy, and how they thought that kind of worthiness should be rewarded, just take your Bibles and look at the 7th chapter of Luke. You there read, *When He had completed all His discourse in the hearing of the people, He went to Capernaum. And a centurion's slave, who was highly regarded by him, was sick and about to die. When he heard about Jesus, he sent some Jewish elders asking Him to come and save the life of his slave. When they came to Jesus, they earnestly implored Him* – now, just listen – *saying, "He is worthy for You to grant this to him."* Yes, that was the Jews' idea of the reason why Jesus should come: because the Centurion was "worthy."

What made him worthy? *For he loves our nation and it was he who built us our synagogue.* He was not worthy because he was a sinner. Oh, no; not at all. But he was worthy, because he *built us our synagogue.* Ha! that was the same old story. It is the story of the present day. There is a great deal of that now. Give that man the most prominent place in the church; let him have the best pew and the one furthest up in the church, because he is "worthy." He has built the church perhaps, or he has endowed a seminary. No matter where his money came from. He may have obtained it by gambling in stocks, or doing something else of a like character; but he has given us this. Oh yes, he is worthy. He may have even made his enormous gains by distilling whiskey. Make room for him, he has a diamond ring on his finger. Make room for her, she wears a grand dress. So said the Jews: "Now, Lord, come at once, for he hath built us a synagogue. Oh, he is worthy. You must not refuse or halt; you must come at once." That was the Jews' idea, and it is the idea of the world today.

But how do you expect to get grace in that way? The moment you base it on the ground of being worthy of it, then to receive it would not be grace at all. It would only amount to this: if the Lord would give a man grace because He owed it to him, He would only be paying a debt. In this instance, however, Jesus went with them to teach them a lesson. Luke goes on to say: *Now Jesus started on His way with them; and when He was not far from the house, the centurion sent friends, saying to Him, "Lord, do not trouble Yourself further, for I am not worthy for You to come under my roof."* That is the kind of humility we want; that is the kind of man we are hunting after – a man that is not worthy. See how quickly he will be saved now that he is in that frame of mind. I suppose that someone had run in to tell this Centurion that Jesus was approaching the house. The Centurion then sent word to Jesus, saying he was not worthy that He should come unto him: *Lord, I am not worthy for You to come under my roof, but just say the word, and my servant will be healed* (Matthew 8:8).

This Centurion had faith at any rate. If he thought himself unworthy to come to Jesus, he sent friends whom he considered better than himself. How common it is to think yourself good and all other people bad! It is pleasant to see a man consider himself a poor, unworthy man. *Lord, I am not worthy for You to come under my roof, but just say the word, and my servant will be healed.* Thank God, he had faith. In this case, because he had faith, Jesus healed his servant without going to him at all. He did not need to go to the house, examine his pulse, and see his tongue. Nor did He have to write out a prescription and send it to the drug store. He simply willed it, and the servant lived.

The Centurion's message continued thus: *For I also am a man under authority, with soldiers under me; and I say to this one, "Go!" and he goes, and to another, "Come!" and he comes, and to my slave, "Do this!" and he does it. Now when Jesus heard this, He marveled* (only twice, I think, is it said that Jesus marveled. He marveled at the unbelief of the Jews [Mark 6:6], and again, at the faith of the Centurion) *and said to those who were following, "Truly I say to you, I have not found such great faith with anyone in Israel."*

Here is a Gentile, He said in effect, here is a man not of the seed of Abraham, and yet what faith he shows! Why, here is a Roman Centurion, and he has more faith than the chosen people of God! Jesus granted the petition at once. When He saw a genuine check presented for payment, He cashed it at once. He pays instantly in the gold of Heaven, without any hesitation or discount. *When those who had been sent returned to the house, they found the slave in good health.* He had been at the point of death one minute; the next, he was made perfectly well.

You may be made whole too, friends. You may even be on the borders of hell and yet may be made inhabitants of the Kingdom of Heaven. Think of this, you men that are the slaves of strong drink. You may be mangled and bruised by sin, but the grace of God can save you. He is the God of all grace (1 Peter 5:10). I hope that grace will flow into your souls tonight.

Christ is the sinner's Friend. If you have read your Bibles carefully, you will see that Christ always took the side of the sinner. Of course, He came down on the hypocrites, and well He might. He took sides against those haughty Pharisees; but where a poor, miserable, humble, penitent sinner came to Him for grace, he always found it. You always read that He deals in grace. Tonight, He will have mercy upon you that confess your sins to Him. If you want to be saved, come right straight to Him. He comes to deal in grace; He comes to bless. Why don't you let Him? Let Him bless you now! Let Him take your sins away now!

A man said to me the other night, "I feel I have to do something." I said to him, "If this grace is unmerited and free, what are you going to do?" And I warn you tonight my friends, against trying to accomplish your own salvation. It really is a question whether this does not keep more people out of the kingdom of God than anything else.

While preaching in Newcastle one night, I said that grace was free; that all were to stop trying to be saved. A woman came down and said to me: "Oh, how wretched I am. I have been trying to be a Christian, and yet you have been telling me tonight not to try." "Has that made you wretched?" I asked. "Yes. If I stop trying, what will become of me?" I said: "But if grace is free, what are you going to do? You cannot get it by working." She replied, "I can't understand it."

Well, let me call your attention now to a few passages of Scripture. I turn to the 2nd chapter of Ephesians and the 8th and 9th verses: *For by grace you have been saved through faith; and that not of yourselves, it is the gift of God; not as a result of works, so that no one may boast.*

Salvation is a gift from God. If a man could earn it, he would boast of what he had done, saying, "Oh, I did it." A Scotchman once said it took two persons to effect his salvation: "God gave me His grace, and I fought against Him." It is not then for men to work for salvation, or they would boast of it, and so rob Christ of His glory. The Ethiopian cannot change his skin, neither can the leopard change his spots. We do not work to win salvation, but we work it out after we have it. If we are ever saved, it must be by grace alone. If you pay anything for salvation, it ceases to be a gift. But God is not down here selling salvation. And what have you to give Him if He was? What do you suppose you would give? Ah, we are bankrupt. "The gift of God is eternal life;" that is your hope. *He who does not enter by the door into the fold of the sheep, but climbs up some other way, he is a thief and a robber* (John 10:1).

Now, who will take salvation tonight? Oh, you may have it if you will. *Now to the one who works, his wage is not credited as a favor, but as what is due* (Romans 4:4). The difference between Martha and Mary was that Martha was trying to do something for the Lord, and Mary was just taking something from Him as a gift. He will smile upon you if you just take grace from Him. It is *to the one who does not work, but believes* (Romans 4:5) that blessings come.

After you get to the Cross, then you may work all you can. If you are lost, you go to hell in the full blaze of the gospel. That grace is free to all – to every policeman here, every fireman, every usher, every singer, every man, woman, and child, every reporter, all of you. What more do you want God to do than He has done? Oh, I hope the grace of God will reach every heart here. Oh, be wise, and open the door of your hearts and let in the King of glory. You will be saved when you believe. It is written, *For the grace of God has appeared, bringing salvation to all men* (Titus 2:11). If you are lost, there is one thing you must do, and that is, trample the grace of God under your feet. It will not be because you cannot be saved, but because you will not.

Young man, will you be saved tonight? It is a question for you yourself to settle. If we could settle it for you, we would, but you must believe for yourself. Christ said to that poor sinning woman, *I do not condemn you, either. Go. From now on sin no more* (John 8:11). O sinner, hear those words. Oh, may the grace of God reach your hearts tonight!

CHAPTER 12

THE GRACE THAT BRINGS SALVATION

For the grace of God has appeared, bringing salvation to all men. – Titus 2:11

In my last address, I was speaking on the subject of Grace, and I now propose to continue the same subject. On the last occasion, I brought the subject down as far as the epistle to Titus, wherein it is written that the grace of God hath appeared, brining salvation to all men. Now I want to call your attention to the 5th chapter of Romans and the 20th and 21st verses: *The Law came in so that the transgression would increase; but where sin increased, grace abounded all the more, so that, as sin reigned in death, even so grace would reign through righteousness to eternal life through Jesus Christ our Lord.*

Sin reigns unto death. The penalty of the law of God is death. The person who sins will die (Ezekiel 18:20). There is no use in having a law if there is not a penalty attached to the disobedience of it. Suppose this state, the State of New York, would pass a law that you should not steal or that you should not murder, and put no penalty to the infraction of that law. What would be the use of the law? What would it be good for? Now sin has reigned unto death, but grace has reigned unto eternal life. Grace does not stop with death. It carries us past death – right through the grave, clear over into the Promised Land.

In the closing verses of Deuteronomy, and in the 1st chapter of Joshua, you read that Moses brought the children of Israel down to Jordan. But he could not take them any further. He was the representative of the law, and that is where the Law brings us – to Jordan. Jordan means death, judgment. After bringing them to death and judgment, Moses could not take them any further, but left them there. The law brings us to death, and there it leaves us. It does not give life; it never has given life, and it never can. Sin reigns unto death, but the grace of God has reigned unto eternal life.

So, when Moses had brought the children of Israel down to Jordan and could not go any further, then came Joshua and took the congregation over and away on their journey. The name of Joshua has the same meaning as the name of Jesus. The word means "Savior." And as Joshua led the people through the Jordan, so Jesus will take His people through the dark valley of the shadow of death and bring them into eternal life. When John came, he appeared as the forerunner of grace and of Jesus. He was the last representative of the old dispensation. In that same river of Jordan, John baptized the people who gathered to hear him there. When Christ came, He commenced where John had left off.

There is a great difference between law and grace, and I want you to bear this in mind and keep the distinction between the two separate and clear in your minds. The difference between law and grace is this: law slays a man (Romans 7:11), but grace makes him live; the law takes a man to death and judgment, but Christ comes and quickens him, giving eternal life. Let me repeat it: law leads unto death, but grace to eternal life by Jesus Christ our Lord. Some people are lingering around Sinai yet, around the old dispensation, around the law. You cannot get them away from Horeb. It is better to come to the Mount of Olives, better to come to Calvary.

Now I want to carry you to another portion, the 14th and 15th verses of the 6th chapter of Romans. There it is written: *For sin shall not be master over you, for you are not under law but under grace. What then? Shall we sin because we are not under law but under grace? May it never be.* Bear that in mind: *we are not under law but under grace.* The Lord Jesus came to bring us out from under the law. It is not anymore, "You shall not" do this; "you shall not" do that. That was the law. Under that dispensation, it was, *Do and live* – now it is, *Live and do.* Christ came and says, *If you love Me, you will keep My commandments.* Before that, it was – *You shall not do this or that.* But grace reigns unto eternal life by Him, and if you love Him, you will keep His commandments, and grace will bring you unto everlasting happiness.

Yet, notwithstanding all these plain texts, some will have it that we are not under grace but remain under the law. Now just turn to the 21st chapter of Deuteronomy and the 18th through 20th verses, and you will see what would happen under this law: *If any man has a stubborn and rebellious son who will not obey his father or his mother, and when they chastise him, he will not even listen to them, then his father and mother shall seize him, and bring him out to the elders of his city at the gateway of his hometown. They shall say to the elders of his city, "This son of ours is stubborn and rebellious, he will not obey us, he is a glutton and a drunkard." Then all the men of his city shall stone him to death; so you shall remove the evil from your midst, and all Israel will hear of it and fear.*

A very strange state of things would take place now if we lived under the law. Think of a man in these days taking his son into Madison Square before the Aldermen of New York; and his fellow citizens coming up there and stoning him to death. It would be pretty effectual in breaking up the rum shops and the whiskeyselling saloons of New York. A man takes his son, who is a confirmed drunkard, and kills him, or has him killed – would not that soon put a stop to the buying and selling of this vile whiskey and intoxicating and maddening stuff that is now being dealt out throughout the country. The distillers would have a good deal of whiskey on their hands.

But grace deals differently with men. See the prodigal son. He went away and lived a low and vicious life. He squandered all he had. He was a drunkard and spent his substance on harlots and thieves. How did his father treat him? Did his father take him out and have him stoned to death? No. That would have been his end under the law I have read to you; but see how his father acted towards him under grace. He met him with a kiss and treated him with kindness and love. The law says, "Stone him," but grace says, "Forgive him."

When Moses was in Egypt, to punish Pharaoh he turned the waters into blood. When Christ was on earth, He turned the water into wine. That is the difference between law and grace. The law says, "Kill him"; grace says, "Forgive him." Law says, "Let him die"; grace says, "Love him." Law makes us crooked; grace straightens us. Law makes us vile; grace cleanses us. That is the difference between law and grace.

When the law came out of Horeb, three thousand men were destroyed (Exodus 32:28). At Pentecost, under grace, three thousand men found life (Acts 2:41). What a difference! When Moses came to the burning bush, he was commanded to take the shoes from off his feet. When the prodigal came home after sinning, he was given a pair of shoes to put on his feet. I would a thousand times rather be under grace than under the law.

Why, the law is a schoolmaster, like a cold, severe man who is continually holding a rattan over you. Well, some of us know what that means. You know what it is to see a rattan and perhaps to feel it. "You shall do this, and you shall not do that." That is the law, with a rattan at the back of it. But under grace, the schoolmaster tries to rule the school with kindness and love. He says, "If you love me, do this; if you love me, do not do that." The schoolmaster that I was taught by was a harsh severe man. It was a word and a blow with him, and generally the blow came first. I knew what it was to have severity in my school days, and I also knew what it was to have kindness. After that stern schoolteacher came a kindhearted lady, who commenced to rule by love.

Well, we thought we would have a grand time – do just as we pleased; we did not fear her. The first time that I broke through a rule, instead of seeing a rattan in her hand, I saw tears in her eyes. That was a good deal worse than a stick or a cowhide to me. She asked me to remain after school. And when we were alone, she took me by the hand and talked to me in a low kind voice with the tears in her eyes. "If you love me," she said, "keep my rules." I tell you, I never broke a rule after that. Her kind words went straight to my heart.

But take a further view of this difference between law and grace. Here is a boy in school, and the master's name is Mr. Law. He holds his cane over him and says, in a cold, severe tone, "You shall not do this, and you shall not do that." This goes on for some time, and there is no love or affection between the boy and his teacher. But by and by, the headmaster comes and takes the pupil out of that room and puts him in another class, the teacher of which is Mr. Grace. The boy, you see, cannot be in both rooms at the same time – cannot have both teachers at the same time.

Now, we are not under law but under grace, and all the Lord wants is to deal in grace and bring us out from the curse of the law. He wants to deal in love with everyone. Thank God, I am not under the law tonight but under grace. And, as I said before, the Lord Jesus is trying to reach every man by grace.

A friend of mine, the last time I was in England, told me this story and gave me the following striking illustration of grace. "Suppose," said he, "that a man has a beautiful farm on the side of the mountain. Everything is within an enclosure. He has a great wall all around it. Everything within the walls is bright and green, while everything outside is hot and dried up. One day, there comes a messenger to the man who has the beautiful farm, and says to him: 'Sir, you have a beautiful flourishing farm, but I want to make it better. I will increase its fertility; I will make it a thousand times better than it now is.'" "No," says the farmer, "my farm is good enough: you can do nothing to better it," and drives him away. He will not have his farm made better, and he builds his walls still higher to keep all men out.

Up in the mountain near the house is a fountain. Its stream is used to irrigate and beautify the farm, and from it, the crystal waters come to the garden. And the one who sent to him says to himself, "This man will not let me make his garden more beautiful; he will not accept my kindness. I will build up a wall and cut off the stream." When the wall arose around the fountain's head, the waters ceased to flow to the farm; the flowers began to fade and wither, and soon everything presented the appearance of desolation and ruin.

So the Lord of Glory comes and wants to give us His grace, but we spurn it, refuse to accept His blessing, and we perish. Christ had difficulty in teaching this doctrine, even to His apostles. When the Jews were offered grace, they would not have it. They would not keep grace in their country. They built up a wall of unbelief; the stream of grace ceased to flow to them, and what was the result? The garden that once was there is now the only dried up and withered spot on the whole mountain round about. Grace has flowed out to the Gentiles and to all the nations, and what a blessing it has been! It was just because the Jews built up a wall of unbelief. That is just what the sinner is doing now. But if you will only let the grace flow, nothing can hinder you from getting a blessing.

And now the question comes: How are we to become partakers of this grace? In the 4th chapter of Hebrews and 16th verse, we read: Therefore let us draw near with confidence to the throne of grace, so that we may receive mercy and find grace to help in time of need. God wants us to come and get all the grace we need. The reason why there are so many halfstarved Christians is because they do not come to the throne of grace. It is related of Alexander that he gave one of his generals, who had pleased him, permission to draw on his treasurer for any sum. When the draft came in, the treasurer was scared, and would not pay it till he saw his master. And when the treasurer told him what he had done, Alexander said, "Don't you know that he has honored me and my kingdom by making a large draft?" So, we honor God by making a large draft on Him. If there is a drunkard here who wishes to get control of his appetite, all he has to do is to come and get all the grace he needs. You can get enough to overcome every temptation.

When Dr. Arnot was in this country – he is now in heaven – I heard him use in a sermon an illustration that impressed me. He said: "Have you not been in a home where the family were at dinner, and have you not seen the old family dog standing near and watching his master, and looking at every morsel of food as if he wished he had it? If his master drops a crumb, he at once licks it up and devours it; but if his master were to set the dish of roast beef down and say, 'Come, come,' he would not touch it. It is too much for him. So with God's children; they are willing to take a crumb, but refuse when God wants them to take the whole platter." God wants you to come right to the throne of grace, and to come boldly.

Some time ago, I learned from the Chicago papers that there had been a run on the banks there, and that many of them were broken. What a good thing it would be to get up a run on the Bank of Heaven! What a glorious thing to get up a run on the throne of grace! God is able to help you and deliver you if you will only come to Him. That is what grace is for.

I want you to turn to the 8th verse of the 9th chapter of 2 Corinthians: *God is able to make all grace abound to you, so that always having all sufficiency in everything, you may have an abundance for every good deed.* I want you to mark that verse. If you have your Bibles with you, draw a mark right round that verse. Many want to know why Christians fail. It is because they do not come to God for grace.

It is not because He has not the ability. Men fail because they try to do too large a business on too small a capital. So with Christians; but God has grace enough and capital enough. What would you think of a man who had one million dollars in the bank, and only drew out a penny a day? That is like you and me, and the sinner is even blinder than we are. The throne of grace is established, and there we are to obtain all the grace we need. Sin is not so strong as the arm of God. He will help and deliver you, if you will come and procure the grace you need.

Now, take all the afflictions that flesh is heir to, and all the troubles and trials of this life, no matter how numerous, and God has grace enough to carry you right through without a shadow. Some people borrow all the trouble they can from the past and the future, and then multiply it by ten, and so get a big load and go reeling and staggering under it. If you ask them to help anyone else, they say they cannot. They have enough to do to take care of their own; forgetting, *Casting all your anxiety on Him, because He cares for you* (1 Peter 5:7).

A man was once travelling along a highway, and overtaking

one carrying a heavy burden on his back, he asked him to ride. But the man, after he had taken a seat, still supported his bundle, saying, "I am willing to carry it if I can only get a ride." So many are content to be nominal Christians, and go along with great loads and burdens! What is the throne of grace for, but to help you carry your burden? God says, "Come," and "As your days so shall your strength be." I suppose we all have thorns in the flesh. Instead of praying to God to take the thorns out, let us pray for grace to bear them. Let us live day by day, casting our care on God.

In the fifth chapter of Romans, there are these precious words: peace for the past, grace for the present, glory for the future. Some think that when they get to Calvary, they have gained all. They have only just commenced. By and by, we shall see the King in His beauty. The glory is on beyond.

A man said to me some time ago, "Moody, do you have grace to go to the stake as a martyr?" I replied, "No. What do I want to go to the stake for?" Someone else asked me, "Moody, if God would take your son, do you have grace to bear it?" I said, "What do I want grace for? I do not want grace to bear that which has not been sent. If God should call upon me to part with my boy, He would give me strength to bear it." What we want is grace for the present, to bear the trials and temptations for every day. "As your days so will your strength be."

The woman who had lost her husband went to Elisha with a story that would move the heart of Elisha or anyone else (2 Kings 4:1-7). Her husband had died a bankrupt, and she feared they would sell her boys into slavery. She came to Elisha and told her story. He asked her what she had with which to pay. She replied, "A pot of oil." Elisha told her to go home, "borrow vessels not a few; take oil, and pour into the empty vessels." Men in these times would not believe in this. They would say, "What, take a pot of oil and pour into all these vessels! What good will that do?" Not so this poor widow. She had faith, and did as she was told. She went to her neighbors and asked for vessels; they could lend her a few. She took all they had and went on. She cleared out the next house, and the next, and the next.

"Borrow," said the prophet, and she went on until her house was filled with vessels. "Now close the doors," she said to her sons. And she poured oil into the first vessel and filled it full, and the next, and the next, and the next, in the same way. She poured it in, and poured it in, and the boys ran and got more vessels, until the house was full of oil. Then she went to Elisha and asked what she should do. He told her, "Go, sell the oil, and pay your debt." Now, Christ pays the debt and gives us enough to live on besides. He not merely pays our debt. He gives us enough to live on. He gives according to our need. "As your days so will your strength be."

Rowland Hill tells a story of a rich man and a poor man of his congregation. The rich man came to Mr. Hill with a sum of money which he wished to give to the poor man, and asked Mr. Hill to give it to him as he thought best, either all at once or in small amounts. Mr. Hill sent the poor man a fivepound note with the endorsement: "More to follow." Every few months came the remittance, with the same message: "More to follow." Now, that is grace. "More to follow" – yes, thank God, there is more to follow. Oh, wondrous grace!

That the grace of God may reach every heart in this assembly tonight – is my earnest prayer.

CHAPTER 13

FAITH IN CHRIST

Faith is the substance of things hoped for, the evidence of things not seen. – Hebrews 11:1, KJV

I want to call your attention on this occasion to the subject of *faith*. I think I hear some of you say: "That is a very dull subject; if I had known that would be the subject, I would not have come." But it is a very important subject. It is faith that brings the blessing after all.

Someone has said there are three things to faith: knowledge, assent, laying hold. Knowledge! A man may have a good deal of knowledge about Christ, but that does not save him. I suppose Noah's carpenters knew as much about the ark as Noah did, but they perished miserably, nevertheless, because they were not in the ark. A good many men know a good deal about Christ, but they are not saved by it. Our knowledge about Christ does not help us if we do not act upon it. But knowledge is very important. Knowledge; assent; then, laying hold. It is that last clause that saves, that brings the soul and Christ together. The best definition I can find of faith is: "Dependence upon the veracity of another." The Bible definition in the 11th chapter of Hebrews is, *Faith is the substance of things hoped for, the evidence of things not seen.* In other words, faith says "Amen" to everything that God says. Faith takes God without any "Ifs." If God says it, faith says, "I believe it." Faith says "Amen" to it.

But now the question is, in whom shall we have faith? A man rose up in one of our young men's meetings the other night and wanted to know why there were so many who had backslidden. One reason for backsliding is because men are not sound in their faith; it is because they have not really been converted to God. A good many men are converted to a church; they say, "I like that church; it is a beautiful church, and there is beautiful singing. I like that quartette choir and the grand organ, and there is a good minister." And so they are converted to the church, and they are converted to the singing, and converted to the organ, and converted to the minister, or they are converted to the people who go there. They get into good society by going there. But that is not being born of God or being converted to God.

Once, there was an old man sitting down among some soldiers, who were telling stories of adventure. One got up and told all about how he had backslidden, but the old soldier said, "I think there is some mistake. The truth of the matter is that you have never yet slid forward."

If a man has faith in the Lord Jesus Christ, he has something to which he can anchor, and the anchor will hold. When the hour of temptation comes, and the hour of trial comes, the man will stand firm. If we are only converted to man and our faith is in man, we shall certainly be disappointed. How often we hear a man say, "There is a member of the church who cheated me out of five dollars; I am not going to have anything more to do with people who call themselves Christians." But if the man had really possessed faith in Jesus Christ, you do not suppose he would have had his faith shattered because someone cheated him out of five dollars, do you? What we want is for men to have faith in the Lord Jesus Christ.

Turn to the prophecy of Jeremiah, 17th chapter, 5th verse: *Thus says the Lord, "Cursed is the man who trusts in mankind and makes flesh his strength, and whose heart turns away from the Lord."* In contrast to this, we have in the 7th verse: *Blessed is the man who trusts in the Lord and whose trust is the Lord.* But "Cursed be the man that trusts in man." That is the reason why so many people are all the time being disappointed, and why there are so many who find their faith shaken: it is because they have been trusting in man, and man has failed them. They have been trusting in themselves; men's hearts are deceitful and desperately wicked, and we cannot have trust in ourselves. And because man has failed us, or because we have failed ourselves, we think God will fail us. But if we put our trust in the God of Jacob, verily He will not fail us.

Faith is very important. You talk about financial panic. If businessmen lost faith among themselves and in each other, how quickly all business would go to the wall! It is the foundation of society. It is the foundation of everything.

Some people think that when we talk about faith in Christ, it must be some miraculous faith; that they have to wait until it comes down out of heaven; that it is some shock which is to come upon them. But this faith in Christ is the same kind of faith that men have in one another. If a man has faith in the God of Jacob, God will never disappoint him. In all my life, I never yet have seen a man whose faith God has disappointed.

There are men who say it does not make any difference what a man believes, if he is in earnest, if he is sincere in his belief. We often hear people ask, "You do not think it makes any difference what kind of belief a man has, if he is only sincere in it, do you?" But oh, my friends, I tell you, it makes all the difference in the world whether a man believes a truth or a lie. If the devil can make you believe a lie, and that you are going to be saved because you are sincere in your belief in it, that is all he wants. Do not suppose for a moment that it does not make any difference what you believe or what your faith is, so that you are only sincere. Do not be deceived by that terrible illusion, which is one of the devil's lies.

Once, there were a couple of men arranging a balloon ascent. They thought they had two ropes fastened to the car, but only one of them was secured. As they unfastened that one rope, the balloon started upward. One of the men seized hold of the car, and the other seized hold of the rope. Up went the balloon, and the man who seized hold of the car went up with it, and was lost. There is just as much reason to say that the man who laid hold of the car would be saved because he was sincere, as the man who believed a lie because he is sincere in his belief. I like a man to be able to give a reason for the faith that is in him.

I once asked a man what he believed, and he said he believed what his church believed. I asked him what his church believed, and he said he supposed his church believed what he did, and that was all I could get out of him. And so men believe what other people believe, and what their church believes, without really knowing what their church and other people do believe.

We must know distinctly in whom we believe. Jesus Christ tells us to have faith in God (Mark 11:22). If we have faith in God, it will carry us through all darkness, and storms, and afflictions, and troubles, and trials. If our faith is in churches, and dogmas, and creeds, and men, and in this thing or that, we shall get into trouble and difficulty before we get through our pilgrim journey. But for him who has faith in God, the light will shine brighter and brighter until he comes at last into the glory of the perfect day.

Some people put their faith in a man. Some say, "There is such and such a minister; I have confidence in him and in his Christianity." They pin their faith to a good man. Sometimes the good man deviates a little, and the one who imitates him thinks that he can, in this little deviation, follow his pattern. He says, "If so and so can do it I can do it," and thus he deviates a little more, and a little more, until he is at last very far away from the moorings.

If a teacher instructs a child in writing, he teaches him to imitate the copy as closely as he possibly can. In the 11th chapter of Hebrews, there is enumerated a long line of Bible heroes of the olden time – men of whom the world was not worthy. In that roll of the faithful are named Abraham, Isaac, and Jacob, and many others of whom time would fail us to tell. But in the next chapter, the writer takes the eye away from the contemplation of these ancient worthies, and says, Look unto Jesus (Hebrews 12:2, KJV).

You need not look at Abraham, or Isaac, or Jacob, but look unto Jesus, the author and finisher of faith. Look to Him alone. Let us learn the lesson that we are not to pin our faith to good men; we are not to place supreme trust in them. They cannot save us. We are to have confidence in them, but when it comes to the great question of salvation, we are to have faith in God, and in God alone. You are not even to obey good men; you are to obey God, and Him only. If God tells us to do a thing, we are to do it. If He tells us to believe a thing, we are to believe it: we are to have faith in God. "Have faith in God." And if God tells you to believe a thing, believe it, and you will have peace, and confidence, and joy. We are to have faith. Christ says, "Have faith in God."

But I hear a great many people saying, "How am I to get this faith? I would come to Christ, but I don't know how to get faith." It would take months and years to get that. Now, I was a long time getting faith. I was anxious to work for the Lord, but I wanted faith. I wanted to get faith, but I went about it the wrong way. I prayed for it and did nothing else. To pray for faith and neglect the Word of God is not the way to obtain faith. The way to obtain faith is to know who God is; and I never knew a man or woman well acquainted with God who wanted faith.

Someone said to a Scotch woman, "You are a woman of great faith." "No," she says, "I am a woman of little faith, but I have a great God." Now just turn for a moment to the 20th chapter of the Gospel of John and the 31st verse: *These have been written so that you may believe that Jesus is the Christ, the Son of God; and that believing you may have life in His name.*

The whole Gospel of John was written for one purpose. John took up his pen and he wrote that Gospel that we might believe that Jesus Christ was the Son of God, and that by believing we might have eternal life. And so, instead of praying for faith, and mourning because we have not faith, let us study the Word of God and get acquainted with the God of Israel. Then we will have faith in Him. If a man or woman is really acquainted with God, such a one will have strong faith in Him. The reason infidels will not trust Him is because they do not know Him.

Turn to the 10th chapter of Romans and the 17th verse: *Faith comes from hearing, and hearing by the word of Christ.* Faith cometh by hearing, and hearing by the Word of God! Now, sinner, do you want to be saved tonight? "Have faith in God." Take Him at His word! Believe what He says. Believe the record God has given of His Son!

I can imagine some of you saying, "I want to, but I have not the right kind of faith." What kind of faith do you want? The idea that you want a different kind of faith is altogether wrong. Use the faith you have; just believe on the Lord Jesus Christ. Moreover, you cannot give any reason for not believing. If a man told me he could not believe me, I would have a right to ask him why he could not believe me. I would have a right to ask him if I had ever broken my word with him; and if I had not broken my word with him, he ought to believe me. I would like to ask you, has God ever broken His word? Can you come forward and tell me that our God has ever failed to keep His word? Never, my friends. He will keep His word.

Unbelief is the sin for which the world will be condemned (John 3:18-19). God condemns the world because they believe not on Jesus; that is the ground of their condemnation (John 3:36; 1 John 5:10). Do not get caught by the terrible delusion that unbelief is a misfortune. Unbelief is not a misfortune, but is the sin of the world (John 16:9). Christ found it on all sides. When He rose from the grave, He found that His disciples doubted. He had reason to cry out against unbelief. Thomas doubted, and so did others of the disciples (Matthew 28:17). It is unbelief which is keeping back God's blessing. I believe we would have a great revival, and thousands of persons would be converted if we only had faith in God.

God is able to do great things if we only believe in Him. Let us have faith. Do not be looking to see if you have the right kind of faith, but see that you really have hold of Christ. Faith is just the hand that reaches out and takes the blessing. Faith sees a thing in God's hand. Faith says, "I will have it."

I see a book in the hand of a gentleman on this platform; I go and take it; I have faith that he will let me have it. Now, my friends, have faith in God tonight. Faith is an outward look, not an inward look. A great many people are looking at their feelings; a great many people are looking at themselves. Do not be looking at your feelings, but look at heaven. Suppose a man who had been in the habit of meeting in the street one whom he had known for years as a beggar were to see him tonight with a nice suit of clothes on and were to accost him with "Hello, beggar," and he were to answer, "Don't call me a beggar; I am no beggar." "But are you not a beggar?" "No, Sir, I am not a beggar." "What is the reason you are not a beggar?" "Why, I was sitting there today and I put out my hand and asked a man to give me something. A gentleman came along, and put five thousand dollars right into my hand." "How do you know it is good money?" "I took it to the bank." "How did you get it?" "I put my hand out, and he just put it in my hand." "How do you know it is the right kind of a hand?" "Oh, pooh, what do I care what kind of a hand it was?"

And so, we have only to reach out the hand of faith tonight and take God's Son. The gift of God is His Son, and this Son is eternal life. Do you want it? *Take it.* Who will have faith in Him tonight? You must have a poor opinion of God if you will not trust Him. I can imagine some people saying, "Oh, we have a great respect for God, but we have not faith in Him." How if your children would say, "Oh, we love papa so much, but we have not faith in him?" You smile at that, and yet how many Christians talk in that way! Oh, this miserable, wretched unbelief! What grounds have we for not believing God?

Let us ask God tonight to take away this unbelief. Let us put our whole confidence in God, and let us trust Him now. If we do not believe Him, John says, we "make Him a liar," and that is what unbelief does. Many a man has been knocked down in the streets of New York for calling another a liar. Men take it as a great insult. When a man tells God that He lies, he insults God. The devil said God was a liar, and men rather believe him than believe God. God is truth. Let us trust Him with all our hearts.

There is a verse here to which I would like to call attention – a brother spoke of it to the inquirers at the inquiry meeting – the 3rd chapter of John and the 33rd verse: *He who has received His testimony* ("His," that is, God's testimony) *has set his seal to this, that God is true.*

In the old days, men used to wear a ring, a signet ring. Instead of signing their names to a document, they would take their ring and with it affix their seal, and so Christ uses that as an illustration. Christ says if you will set to your seal that God is true, He will believe it. You then set to your seal that God is true. Oh, lay hold of that verse tonight: *He who has received His testimony has set his seal to this, that God is true.*

Who will endorse Him? Who will believe? Faith says, "I will. I will set to my seal that God is true." Is there not someone here who will set to his seal that God is true? If some here will do that, there will be joy in heaven tonight. Is there not someone who will do it?

I once told my little Willie to jump off a high table, and I would catch him. But he looked down and said, "Papa, I'm afraid." I again told him I would catch him, but he looked down and said, "Papa, I'm afraid." You smile, but that is just the way with the unbeliever. He looks down and dares not trust the Lord. You would say that would be blind faith, but I say it would not be. I told Willie to look at me and then jump, and he did it and was delighted. He wanted to jump again, and finally his faith became so great that he would jump when I was eight or ten feet away, and cry out, "Papa, I'm comin'." I remember seeing a man in Mobile putting little boys on the fence posts, and they jumped into his arms with perfect confidence. But there was one boy, nine or ten years old, who would not jump. I asked the man why it was, and he said the boy was not his. Ah, that was it. The boy was not his. He had not learned to trust him. But the other boys knew him and could trust him.

Oh, sinner, will you not acquaint yourself with Christ tonight, and spring into the arms of a loving Savior? He will keep you. Who will believe in the Lord Jesus Christ tonight? Who will come to Him and be saved? Will you not take God at His word? May He give you strength and faith tonight to trust Him, as Job did.

CHAPTER 14

THE COMPASSION OF CHRIST

Jesus . . . was moved with compassion.
– Matthew 14:14, KJV

I want to call your attention this evening to just one word – compassion. Some time ago I took up the concordance and ran through the life of Christ to see what it was that moved Him to compassion; for we read that often in His life, while down here, He was moved with compassion. I was deeply profited in my own soul, as I ran through the record of His life and found those passages of Scripture that tell us of His being moved with compassion. In the 14th chapter of Matthew and 14th verse, we find these words: Jesus went forth, and saw a great multitude, and was moved with compassion toward them, and He healed their sick. And in another place, we read that He was curing those who had need of healing (Luke 9:11).

There was no need for anyone to tell Him what was in the hearts of the people. When I stand before an audience like this, I cannot read your history, but He knew the history of each one. In one place in Scripture (Proverbs 14:10), it is written, The heart knows its own bitterness; but when Christ stood before a multitude such as this, He knew the particular bitterness in each heart. He could read every man's biography; He knew the whole story. As He stood before that vast multitude, the heart of the Son of God was moved with compassion, just as in the preceding verses we find Him to have been when John's disciples had come to Him with their sad story and with broken hearts (see verse 12.) Their beloved master had been beheaded by the wicked king; they had just buried the headless body, and then they came to Jesus to tell all their sorrow to Him. It was the best thing they could do. No one could empathize with them as Jesus could; no one had the same compassion for them that Jesus had. In all our troubles, the best thing we can do is to follow in the footsteps of John's disciples and tell it all to Him. He is a High Priest who can be touched with the feeling of our infirmities (Hebrews 4:15). A little while after this, Jesus too had to suffer death. He knew that shortly He too would lay down His life, but He did not think of that as He looked upon the multitude, and His heart was moved with compassion. He sought to do them good; He gladly healed their sick.

In the 1st chapter and 41st verse of Mark, there is a narrative that brings out the compassion of Christ. A leper came to Him, and when Jesus saw him, His heart was moved with compassion. The poor creature was "full of leprosy" from head to foot (Luke 5:12). I can just imagine how the leper told his whole story to Christ, and it was the very best thing he could do. He had no friends to be interested for him; he might have had a wife and family, or a loved mother, but they could not be there to plead for him. The law forbade anyone speaking to him or touching him, but undoubtedly someone had one day come out and lifted up his voice and told him that a great prophet had arisen in Israel, who could cure him of the leprosy – that it was quite certain He could do it, because He had performed miracles equal to that, and that He could give him healing if he would only ask Him.

This leper told his sad story. Let us bring that scene down to our own day. Suppose that anyone in this assembly here tonight would find that he was a leper, and that the law required him to leave his home, family, and friends. What a scene it must have been when that poor leper left his home, left the wife of his bosom, left his own offspring, with the thought that he was never to see them again! It was worse than death; he had to go into a living sepulcher, to go forth from home, wife, mother, father, children, friends, and live outside the walls of the city. And while he was out there, if any man would come near him, he had to cry, "Unclean! Unclean! Unclean!" He had to cover his upper lip and rend his garments, so that all men would know him.

There outside the walls of the city, the leper might be seen. It might happen in the course of years that someone came out and shouted at the top of his voice and told him that his little child was dying; but he could not go to see his dying child or comfort his wife in her affliction. There in exile, he had to remain, banished from home, while his body was rotting with that terrible disease, with no loved friends to care for him. That was the condition of the poor leper. And when he heard that Jesus could cure him, he went to Him and said, *Lord, if You are willing, You can make me clean* (Luke 5:12). And Jesus was moved with compassion, and He put forth His hand and touched him. The law forbade His doing this – forbade anyone touching him; but that great heart was moved, and He touched the man, and the moment He touched him, the leprosy was gone. He was healed that very moment. He went forth and recounted again and again what a great blessing had come to him.

Did you ever stop to think that the leprosy of sin is a thousand times worse than that Eastern leprosy? All that it could do was to destroy the body. It might eat out the eye, it might eat off the hand, it might eat off the foot – but think of the leprosy of sin! It brought angels from heaven, from the highest heights of glory down not only into this world, but into the very pit of hell. Satan once lifted up high hallelujahs in heaven, but sin brought him out of heaven down into his realm of darkness.

Look into the home of the drunkard; look into the home of the libertine; look into the home of the harlot; look into the homes of those who are living in sin! The leprosy of sin is a thousand times worse than the Eastern leprosy of the body. But if the poor sinner, all polluted with sin, will come to Christ and say, after the fashion of this poor leper of whom we have just read, "Lord, You can have compassion upon me; You can take away this desire for sin; if You will, You can save me" – He will save such a one tonight.

Oh, sinner, you had better come to Him; He is the very best friend that you have. It is Jesus, the Son of God, whom we preach here tonight. He has come to help you; He stands in this assembly now. We cannot see Him with the bodily eye, but we can with the eye of faith, and He will save every sinner who will come to Him tonight. My dear friends, will you not come to Him and ask Him to have mercy and compassion upon you?

If I were an artist, I would like to paint that scene and bring out vividly that poor filthy leper coming to the Son of God, and the Son of God reaching out His hand and touching and cleansing him.

And if I were an artist, there is another picture I would like to draw, and hang up on yonder wall, that you might see it: that is, of the father who came to Christ with his beloved boy, his only child (Luke 9:38). Jesus had been up on the mount of transfiguration with Peter, James, and John, and there He had met Elijah the prophet and Moses the lawgiver. Heaven and earth had there met together. On that memorable night, the Father's voice from out the overshadowing cloud had declared the preciousness of the Beloved Son.

In the morning when the Lord came down from that hill of glory, a great multitude welcomed Him. Among that crowd were the anxious father and the afflicted boy who was possessed of an evil spirit. The father told the pitiful story, and how the disciples had failed to cast out the evil spirit from the young man. No one but a father can understand how much that man loved that boy; his heart was wrapped up in that child. Yet the boy was not only deaf and dumb but was possessed with a devil, and sometimes this devil would throw him into the fire and sometimes into the water (Mark 9:17-25; Matthew 17:15). When the father came to Jesus, He said to him, Bring him here to Me. And when he was coming, the devil cast him down to the ground. So every man on his way to Christ must first be cast down. There he lay foaming, wallowing, and Jesus only said, How long has this been happening to him? From childhood, was the answer. The father goes on speaking somewhat in this way: "Oh, you do not know how much I have suffered with this boy! When a child, he was grievously tormented; he has well-nigh broken my heart." Some of you here perhaps have children who are suffering from some terrible disease and are breaking your hearts – you can sympathize with that father. How that father wept when he brought that poor boy! And when Jesus saw that pitiful scene, His heart was moved with compassion. With a word, He cast out the devil. I can see the boy coming home with his father, leaping and singing and praying.

Let us learn a lesson. Mother, father, do you have a son of whom the devil has taken possession of? Bring him to Jesus. He delights to bless. All you have to do is to take such a one in the arms of your faith and bring him to Jesus.

I want to call your attention to a difference between the father we read of in the 9th chapter of Mark and the poor leper in the 8th chapter of Matthew. The leper says: *If You are willing, You can make me clean.* There was the "if" in the right place. The other said: *If You can do anything, take pity on us.* He puts the "if" in the wrong place. The Lord said, *All things are possible to him who believes.* Let us believe that the Son of God can save our sons and our daughters. Oh, have you a poor drunken son? Have you a poor brother who is a slave to strong drink? Come, bring him to the meeting here tomorrow night, and let your cry be, "Lord, have compassion on my darling boy, and save him," or "Lord, have mercy on my poor sinful brother."

There was a great number of disciples gathered around Jesus as He was going near the little city of Nain. And what met His eyes? A dead man was being carried out. I cannot help but think of that event. When I was preaching to the men last Sunday night, a poor man fell dead. He was carried out while we were preaching. And here, a young man was being carried out of the city of Nain, dead, and a great number of his friends accompanied the widow to the burial of her only son. He was her "only son," we are told, and his mother was a widow. The father, the head of the house, had died perhaps long before. In the distant past, that mother had probably watched over her husband, until at last, she closed his eyes in death. That was a terrible blow, and now death had come again.

You who are mothers can understand how likely it would be that, through all that sickness, the mother would be unwilling to let the neighbors come in and watch over her only son. For weeks, probably, a light was kept burning in that little cottage in Nain. There is that mother; she is watching over that boy, her only son. How she loves him! You who are mothers can sympathize with her. You who are mothers can enter into full sympathy with her. You can understand how hard it was to lose that only son.

She thinks she will never look into that pleasant face again. She thinks she will never look into those kindly eyes again. They have been closed; she has closed them with her own loving hands. She has imprinted the last kiss upon that loved cheek. Now they lay him in the coffin, or upon the bier, and perhaps four men take him up just as they did the man with the palsy, and they bear him away to his resting place. There is a great multitude coming out of Nain. All Nain is moved. Most likely, the widow was loved very much, and there is a great multitude attending her. And now we see them as they are coming out of the gate of the city. The disciples look, and they see a great crowd coming out of Nain; and the two crowds, the two great multitudes, come together, and the Son of God looks upon the scene.

Twice we read that Jesus sighed (Mark 7:34; 8:12). He had followers on His right hand, followers on His left hand, followers behind Him, and followers before Him. He saw the woe and suffering in this wretched world, and He looked upon that weeping mother. Death had its captive. And will not the Son of God look with pity upon that widow? He saw those tears trickling down her cheeks, and the great heart of the Son of God was moved. He would not suffer that son to pass to the grave. He touched the bier, and the bearers stood still. Jesus spoke the word of power: *Young man, I say to you, arise!* (Luke 7:14) and the dead heard the voice of the Son of God and arose from the dead. I can imagine the youth saying, "Blessed be God, I am alive."

You know, Christ never preached any funeral sermons. Here death had met its Conqueror; and when He spoke the word, away went death. The Son of God was moved with compassion for that poor widow. There is not a poor widow in all the world with whom Christ does not sympathize. You who are widows, mourning over loved ones, let me say to you: Jesus is full of compassion. Let me say, He is the same tonight that He was eighteen hundred years ago when He bound up that poor widow's heart at the gate of Nain. He will comfort you, and that tonight.

If you will just come to Him, and ask Him to bind up your wounded heart, or ask Him to help you to bear your great affliction, the Son of God will do it. You will find that His arm is underneath you to help you carry the burden. There is not a poor, suffering, crushed, bruised heart in all this great city with whom the Son of God is not in sympathy. And He will have compassion on you if you only come home to Him. He will bind up that heart of yours.

Yes, Jesus was moved with compassion when He saw that poor widow. They did not need to tell Him the story; He saw how the heart of the mother was broken, and so He just spoke the word. He did not take that young man with Him. He might have taken him along with Him to glorify Himself, but *Jesus gave him back to his mother* (Luke 7:15). Oh, note the tenderness of that act! He took him right out of the hands of death and handed him back to the mother. Yes, there was a happy home in Nain that night. How surprised the mother must have been; she could hardly have believed her eyes. Oh, my friends, Jesus has the same power tonight, and He will bind up your aching hearts if you will only just come to Him.

Did you ever hear of anyone coming to Christ whom He did not accept? He does not care what position in life you hold. No matter how low down you are, no matter what your disposition has been; you may have been low in your thoughts, words, and actions; you may have been selfish; your heart may be overflowing with corruption and wickedness; yet Jesus will have compassion upon you. He will speak comforting words to you – not treat you coldly nor spurn you, as perhaps those of earth would – but He will speak tender words, and words of love, affection, and kindness. Just come at once.

He is a faithful Friend – a Friend that sticks closer than a brother. He is a brother born for adversity. Treat Him like a brother and like a friend, and you will have a heavenly balm poured upon your wretched, broken heart. He is real. He is tangible. We do not worship a myth; we do not praise an unreal being. He is an everlasting, living Person, a Man sitting at the right hand of God, full of the power and the majesty of heaven. He comes here tonight in the Spirit. He is present with you. Oh, accept Him, and He will deliver you, and save you, and bless you. My friends, just treat Him as if you saw Him here in person, as if He stood here in person the same as I do now. Come to Him then with all your troubles, and He will bless you. If He were here, and you saw Him beckoning to you, you would come, would you not? Well, you would be saved then by sight, but He wants you to take Him by faith.

There are those here tonight who believe He is here now. Mr. Dodge, you came here in Christ's name, did you not? [Mr. Dodge: "Yes."] Is it not Christ's name that has brought you here, Dr. Hepworth? [Dr. Hepworth: "Yes."] And you, Dr. Booth, did you not come here in Christ's name? [Dr. Booth: "Yes."] Yes, you have come here for Christ, and are ready to confess His name. You are witnesses to His name. Yes, here are two or three gathered together in the name of Christ, and He is here, because He has promised so to be. Take Him at His word then, my friends. The Son of God is here tonight. Do you doubt it? Is there a man or woman in this assembly tonight who doubts it? I tell you, He is here. He is here just as truly as if you saw Him. Press up to Him. He is infinite in compassion and will take pity upon you.

Oh, my friends, that raising of the widow's son displayed our Lord's earthly compassion; but what conception can you form of His deep compassion for souls? If you come and tell Him your sad stories, His heart will be moved. Oh, come and tell Him your sin and misery. He knows what human nature is; He knows what poor, weak, frail mortals we are, and how prone we are to sin. He will have compassion upon you. He will reach out His tender hand and touch you as He did the poor leper. You will know the touch of His loving hand. There is virtue and power in it.

A mother received a dispatch saying that her boy had been wounded. She resolved to go down to the front to see him. She knew that the nursing of the hospital would not be as tender as hers would be. After much solicitation, she saw the doctor, and after repeated warnings from him not to touch the boy or to wake him up – he had only a few days to live at any rate, and waking him up would only hasten his death – she went to his bedside. When she saw her poor boy lying there so still and lifeless, with the marks of his suffering so fresh upon him, she could not resist the temptation to lay her hand on his brow. Instinct told him it was his mother's loving hand, and without opening his eyes, he said, "Oh, mother, have you come?"

And I say to all here: Let Jesus touch you tonight. His is a loving, tender hand, full of sympathy and compassion. Oh, my brother [looking at a young man in one of the front rows], will you have Him tonight? You will! Thank God! Thank God! This young man says he will accept Him. We have been praying two or three days for this young man, and now he says he will take Christ. Oh, bless the Lord!

Let us pray, and as we pray, let us make room for Jesus in our hearts, just as this young man has done, upon whom He has had compassion and whom He has saved.

DWIGHT L. MOODY - A BRIEF BIOGRAPHY

Dwight Lyman Moody was born on February 5, 1837, in Northfield, Massachusetts. His father died when Dwight was only four years old, leaving his mother with nine children to care for. When Dwight was seventeen years old, he left for Boston to work as a salesman. A year later, he was led to Jesus Christ by Edward Kimball, Moody's Sunday school teacher. Moody soon left for Chicago and began teaching a Sunday school class of his own. By the time he was twenty-three, he had become a successful shoe salesman, earning $5,000 in only eight months, which was a lot of money for the middle of the nineteenth century. Having decided to follow Jesus, though, he left his career to engage in Christian work for only $300 a year.

D. L. Moody was not an ordained minister, but was an effective evangelist. He was once told by Henry Varley, a British evangelist, "Moody, the world has yet to see what God will do with a man fully consecrated to Him."

Moody later said, "By God's help, I aim to be that man."

It is estimated that during his lifetime, without the help of television or radio, Moody traveled more than one million miles, preached to more than one million people, and personally dealt with over seven hundred and fifty thousand individuals.

D. L. Moody died on December 22, 1899.

Moody once said, "Some day you will read in the papers that D. L. Moody, of East Northfield, is dead. Don't you believe a word of it! At that moment I shall be more alive than I am now. I shall have gone up higher, that is all – out of this old clay tenement into a house that is immortal; a body that death cannot touch, that sin cannot taint, a body fashioned like unto His glorious body. I was born of the flesh in 1837. I was born of the Spirit in 1856. That which is born of the flesh may die. That which is born of the Spirit will live forever."

Did you know...

- We offer 175+ eBooks for free download?
- You can listen to 175+ audiobooks free of charge on YouTube?
- We sell books for only $0.99 each if given away free of charge for ministry?*

www.anekopress.com

*Prices subject to change

www.ingramcontent.com/pod-product-compliance
Lightning Source LLC
LaVergne TN
LVHW012102070526
838200LV00074BA/4010